A
FRESH
Start

NEALIE MILLER

ISBN 979-8-88851-575-4 (Paperback)
ISBN 979-8-88851-576-1 (Digital)

Covenant Books
11661 Hwy 707
Murrells Inlet, SC 29576
www.covenantbooks.com

Acknowledgments

To my readers and to my many friends all over, I hope you will enjoy reading my story as much as I enjoyed writing it. I must say this so that you would understand: my life story was not all pretty and was not all easy to write about. Not only because I enjoy writing, always have, but what motivated me to write my story here is because of where I was in my life at one time—in a dark area, not having a relationship with my Lord and Savior Jesus Christ, and going to a counseling place called Fresh Start, where they helped me get my life back on track. So in writing, I did change a few people's names to protect the real person, out of respect. This story is about me and not about them. I want to thank all of the staff who were at Fresh Start during my time there for their help and walking with me through two years of a real tough time in my life. As you read my story, it might feel at times that I got pretty hard on my counselor, and I did, but just so you know, we also had good times, and today, I still appreciate him and his family as much as anyone. I just want you to be able to see the real picture of my personal struggles of a man who wanted what was right. A man after God's own heart. And when you read my story here, I want you to be able to feel that coming from me. So thank you, staff, for all your input into my life in those two years. Reading the Bible daily became real to me and was my most enjoyable time during my stay at Fresh Start.

To my wonderful wife and children, who stuck with me through the thick and thin as we searched and longed for a real family life. We have learned what it takes to stay strong when we all wanted to fall apart. Today, my wife and I are more in love than we were even through our dating years. To our wonderful children and grandchildren, today, we enjoy every one of them to our fullest. And last but not least, my real hope and desire is that you, my readers, will see there is light at the end of the tunnel when everything looks pretty dark in front of your path. At one time in my life, I could not see any light at the end of the tunnel.

And thank You, Jesus, for setting me free, giving me that hope and peace that I was longing for, for years.

Please enjoy reading, and if you get the urge to, go ahead and write me a letter. My address is in the back of this book.

Chapter 1

Oh, the Perfume

I like to tell people that we dated for three years and only saw each other three times in those three years. I tell people that the young folks these days are really, *really* spoiled. In our home area here in Daviess County, Indiana, even among the Amish, the youngins would think it was just absolutely horrible if they couldn't see each other at least twice a week. If you have never been in Daviess County, Indiana, you should come visit once. Just the same as some people will say they have never been in Holmes County, Ohio. I personally just love Holmes County, Ohio. When I mention Holmes County, I'm referring to the whole surroundings of the Amish area up there. I know there are other counties joining, but to me, Holmes County is Holmes County. But here in Daviess County, Indiana, the land is fairly flat, slightly rolling in some areas. Not as flat as Arthur, Illinois, which is just under three hours west of us. Far from being hilly like Holmes County, Ohio. Farmland, cabinet shops, sawmills, a few dairy farms, cabinet shops, turkey farmers, general stores, grocery stores, cabinet shops, carpenter crews galore, Amish restaurants, truss factories, candy shops, cabinet shops, shoe stores, ice cream shops, mini barn builders, and did I mention cabinet shops? You got it, more cabinet shops than I have a handle on. Daviess County would like to think they are somewhat of a tourist place, but I'm here to tell you right now, nothing compared to the northern part of Indiana like Shipshewana area or Holmes County, Ohio, or Lancaster, Pennsylvania, or others.

Far from it.

When Malinda and I dated, we saw each other three different times in our dating years. I barely even knew what she looked like from one visit to the next. Seriously. I didn't have a photo of her sitting on my dresser that I could look at whenever I wanted. We didn't have a camera to share photos of each other. I had no pictures of her to look at to admire. Just the many handwritten letters she'd send me every week. And those, they were very precious. They were stuffed away in a little chest I kept on the top of my dresser with a small golden padlock. That's it. I didn't want my brothers in there or my parents. They were love letters.

I complained to my dad about not being able to visit much or even getting to know her much, but I guess he didn't think we had the money to travel back and forth like that. Or maybe he didn't think it was that big of a deal, I don't know. I longed to have a connection with my girlfriend, but it was just not possible. Our very first date was the best date we ever had, and it was one that I will never forget for as long as I live or have a good memory. I will tell you more about that special date here in a little bit.

Now, before you jump to all kinds of conclusions of why we didn't see each other more, nope, it was not my thought for ideal dating either, not at all. I would have loved to see her much more often. The fact that we lived so far away from each other made it difficult to see each other much. So we did the best we could with what we had. The next best thing we had was simply writing letters to each other. Our community didn't travel by van or just an ordinary driver to go visit other communities. One of the reasons for this church rule was for just that very reason, so young folks don't make a habit of running to another community to see their special friend every single week. I guess they thought a couple times a year was enough. We had to travel by Greyhound bus, and I thoroughly enjoyed riding the Greyhound. I fell in love with buses at a very young age, which you will see later on in my story here.

So we had to do much writing. I just *loved* receiving those love letters from her in the mail. My heart fluttered for those love letters every week. I wrote her a letter every week, and she wrote me a letter every week. Wednesday was the day the letter was supposed to come in the mail, and that day was *always* a very big highlight day for me, every week.

At the time of this writing, we have now been married for thirty-three years and we have seven healthy children, three boys and four girls. Our two oldest are married, and we have four grandchildren. How awesome and wonderful is God to provide and bless us in this way. Sometime back, I saw a coffee mug with writing on it that read like this:

"To my Wife,"

> I wish I could turn back the clock
> I'd find you sooner and love you
>   longer
> If I could give you one thing in
>   life,
> I would give you the ability
> to see yourself through my eyes
> Only then would you realize
> how special you are to me,
> I love you to the moon and back.

Love, Your Husband

So before I tell you all about our first date and the *best* date we ever had, I need to slow down here a bit and start from the beginning. So here it goes.

The first time that I had ever seen Malinda, she was sitting out in the kitchen on a barstool. I think it was a barstool. At least it was a little stool with no back on it, and it sat a little higher than a regular chair. This was on a Sunday evening after we had church. I was sitting in the living room listening to the stories of older married men. She was no more than sixteen years old, and I remember getting a glimpse of her out there, but to be very honest, I don't recall that it ever entered my mind at that time that this visiting young girl sitting out there in the kitchen might someday become my wife. Looking back, I do remember somewhat that she wasn't a bad-looking girl. To me, she was just another visiting girl in the area that evening who happened to be in our area. She was from Wisconsin, a long way from home. She'd been in the area visiting her brother who was living in our area there in Palmer Square, Ohio. And that is about all I remember of her on this particular visit. At this point, I didn't even think about possibly dating her someday.

So how this all came about then was, sometime later, my uncle who was not yet married at the time found out that she was coming to the area yet once again for a visit. This time, she was going to be seventeen years old and old enough to have a date. I remembered from her previous visit that her name was Malinda, and I remember thinking that that name did have a sweet ring to it. I liked the name. And to this day, I still like that name. Malinda was somewhat an unusual name for our area, and I liked it. The name rang sweet. Not that I was so sure about having a date with her, but my uncle convinced me that I really needed to. My uncle was older; otherwise, I imagine he would've wanted a date with her himself. I would probably not have a chance if he thought he'd had a chance at her. But he was older, which in turn was a benefit to me. I'd get the chance. If I didn't, one of the other boys in the area certainly would and then it might be too late for me. It just so happened that her married brother, whom she was coming to visit, had invited all the church youth over for that following Sunday evening, and this was the evening I was to have a date with this beautiful young girl, if I was to listen to my uncle. I didn't even know the girl yet. Barely remembered what she had looked like from the last time she was around this area. In fact, up until now, I still had never even spoken the first word with her yet. See, back then, the boy that was going to have a date did not actually go ask the young girl out himself. It was always someone else who did the asking. In this case, it was my uncle who wanted the privilege to ask her for me. Yes, I was very nervous and probably as bright as a beet. What if she says no? Then the whole community would come to find out a young visiting girl said *no* to me. That would hurt. And it would not feel good.

By the time she was supposed to have arrived in our area, there had been a death in our community. A young couple had their firstborn baby, and it only lived a couple days and then died. So there was going to be a funeral. As a young teenager, I remember this was a shock to our community. We didn't know the baby even had any health issues. So in the meantime, this young Wisconsin girl showed up and my uncle had already been after me to have a date with her before she ever arrived. He already had the permis-

6

sion from me to ask her if she'd do it to have a date with me. So here we went to the funeral of this little baby, and of course, the Wisconsin girl had arrived already and had also joined our church at the funeral. Of course, she rode with her brother and family to the funeral. Lo and behold, during the funeral service, she sat with the rest of the youth girls on the girls' bench, and she sat dead smack behind me, her knees occasionally touching my back. She later told me she thought I intentionally scooted back so her knees would touch me. I don't remember that, but who knows. Of all days, of all the people at this funeral, and I'm to have a date with this visiting girl, and she sits dead smack behind me. What are the chances of that happening? Seriously?

I was extremely nervous because I figured that my uncle Harvey had already asked her if she would accept a date from me. What if she knew the boy sitting right dead smack in front of her was the one she had said *no* to? I was so embarrassed, I wanted to leave, but I couldn't. After the funeral services, in the afternoon sometime, before we had left the place of the funeral, I asked Harvey if he had already asked her. I was nervous even asking him because I just knew he would say, "Yes, I did ask her, and I'm sorry, unfortunately, she had said no." But when he told me he had not even asked her yet, I will have to say, I was slightly disappointed. I wanted to know her answer.

Talk about being held in suspense. This was going to be a long week. Now I had to wait until Sunday evening when we arrived at the young folks' gathering to find out if she'd accept a date with me. And to my delight, she had said *yes*. Now her name even meant more to me. Somehow, her name now even had a sweet twang to it that it would put the butterflies through my stomach even at the thought of it. Now, folks, this was not your usual date, and I am about to tell you about it. As I write this story of our first dating experience, I've since told it numerous times already on the charter bus as I drive around, and I was told that I needed to write our story in a book someday. So here it goes. Our dating story in itself, I could probably never find enough words to fill a whole book, but with everything that became because of this one date—wow, lots of water has passed under the bridge since then and has a story to tell in itself. It's definitely a love story through the good times and the bad times. God has definitely been gracious in walking right alongside of us all the way through. Well, actually, there may have been times when God had let me go my own way for a spell because of the road I had chosen to go down. But before I go there, I need to tell you about our first date, right?

This was the best date we ever had and one I will never forget. It was very precious to both Malinda and I. That first date was not what I was expecting. Actually, I don't know what I was expecting. Going back a few years though, my very first date *ever* was not with Malinda. It was with a girl from our own youth group who I had known for several years before we were ever old enough to run around with the youth group. I had an eye on this girl for several years already, and I thought I would for sure make her my wife someday. I was just certain of it. I was going to make sure no one else gets her first. I wanted to date her. And I definitely did like her name as well, from the time I had first laid my eyes on her.

When that time came where she was old enough and she started going out with the youth group, I did in fact get the opportunity to ask her for a date. Our first and only date and I simply blew it. I picked her up in front of the house right after our normal Sunday evening youth gathering, and she got on my buggy. I remember wondering if this was a dream come true or was this for real. I was looking for this day for a long time already. The horse took off, and we rode and rode a long, long way to her house, many miles on this rough gravel road. Poor old horse had to pull that buggy for miles and miles over rough gravel road. She lived far out from our community but was still part of our church. Her parents decided to buy land way out there. So we rode many miles, but all in silence, except for the steel-rimmed wheels crunching over the gravel on the road. I was totally, let's see, what would be the correct word for this, starstruck as they would say. My mind went completely blank, and I could not, for the life of me, strike up a conversation with my date. There was just absolutely nothing I could think of to talk about. Afterward, of course, I thought of many things I would have liked to talk to her about, but at that moment, my mind went into numbness. Totally blank.

When we got to her house, I tied up the horse, went inside where we had our date, and we sat there in total silence again. Words would just not come. Totally "date struck." I guess I must have been totally shocked to finally have the opportunity to take this girl home. Home to her house for a date. It was *really* happening. Happening, but without words or a conversation.

When the time was for me to leave for home at midnight, I had only gotten a few words spoken to her and she did the same to me. I'm sure it was the worst night she'd *ever* experienced on a date night. I simply blew my chance on her. It was the most awkward feeling ever. Since then, I have thought back to this evening, and I could think of many things we could have talked about, but the words were stuck in my throat that evening and would not come out. Absolutely would not come out. What a horrible dating experience. It was a total flop.

Now, on to a better date.

So back to the date with Malinda. At 9:30 in the evening, after it was dark and the rest of the youth were hitching up their horses and leaving to go home, I was hiding somewhere out back, pretending I'd done went home already. I didn't want *nobody* to know I was having a date with this Wisconsin girl. I guess I was too embarrassed for others to know. I had this fear within me that this date would be another flop. That it would go the same way as my date with the other girl I had dated earlier on. What was I going to do different, so I wouldn't blow this one?

I wasn't sure. I didn't even personally know this girl yet. I went into hiding. I did not want anyone to know I was having another date night, this time with a different girl. So I was waiting until everyone had done left for home. So I hid out back, hoping everyone else was thinking I'd also done left for home. I didn't need to hitch up a horse this evening because I had walked over from my home just under two miles away. So as far as the others might know, I could have easily left for home on foot already. But for some reason, several of the youth boys seemed to be hanging around there for the longest time, and I started getting nervous they were going to get up the nerve to go in there and ask her out, not knowing she'd done been spoken for. But hey, I done had my ducks all in a row early on already on this one. Once everyone had finally all left, my uncle Harvey who knew where I was hiding out at, came to rescue me. I was very nervous, believe me. I wasn't sure how this was all going to go yet. I was about to meet this young girl in person for a date from Wisconsin whom I never had a word with yet. Looking back now, that is some way to start a date, isn't it? But that was common practice in our area.

In our area when a boy had a date with a girl, it was common for the young couple to go to her parents' house for the date. Tonight, in our case, she was not in her hometown area, so we would have the date at her married brother's place which just so happened was where we had been the whole evening with all the other youth folks, fellowshipping, getting

11

to know each other better, eating, and playing games. So this turned out just great for us. We didn't need to go anywhere. We were already at our dating location. All dates were basically done in the same fashion, at least for this Amish community and the strict rules it had. The boy sits on a rocking chair in the living room and the girl will then sit on his lap, and there they sit until midnight. Once it was midnight, it was time for the boy to make his way home. Both sides of the parents expected this, and it was strictly enforced by the church rules. I really had no problem with that. By the time midnight came around, usually both parties were about ready to call it bedtime anyway. But this young girl that I was having this date with had some very special perfume on her this evening that was just absolutely out of this world. It was addicting. I mean it smelled really, really good. Our first date went really well, and time went really fast. She was a talker, and this helped me out tremendously. If I didn't have anything to say, she did. Being I would probably been more on the shy side again, she had a way to get the shy side of me opened right up and we had the best date ever.

But here is the funny part. I had just under two miles to walk home in the dark alone and a flashlight in hand to flash at anything that made some spooky noises at me during this midnight walk home. If a car came from any direction, I would jump in the ditch and lay flat in the tall grass or run into the cornfield until it had passed. I was not taking any chances for a midnight stalker. But here was the good part while walking home. My hands smelled freshly of this good sweet-smelling perfume she had on her that night. From holding her on my lap all evening up until midnight, it had rubbed off on me, and it stuck. I thought this was just the coolest thing ever. Now, here is where this story had to take a turn for the worst, and I was not happy about it at all. See, I was always the one to milk the one cow every morning and every evening that my parents kept around the farm for our own use of milk. Now, if you have ever milked a cow by hand, I imagine you already know what I'm about to share here. Milking a cow leaves a scent on your hands and your clothes that only a cow can leave. It's that cowy scent type of scent. Well, that next morning, I was going to have to milk the cow, and I knew there was not a chance that this sweet-smelling perfume was having a chance against this cow-milking scent. What a real bummer. What was I going to do about that? Do I play sick and have one of my brothers milk the cow the next morning? Ooh, but I was *not* good at playing sick. I was way too active to lay in bed, pretending to be sick and hearing the others outside enjoying the beautiful sunny day. So this was not even an option. All this good old boy could do was go face the cold, hard, bitter truth and go milk the cow. What's more, I got to thinking once I go to bed and get up the next morning, this good smell on my hands will likely be all gone anyway. So off to bed I went.

All too quickly, the next morning came around with that dreadful rattle our mother always did to get us boys up to get our morning chores done before it was breakfast time. She'd use a broom handle and reach up to the ceiling which had an air ventilator, and she'd whip that handle loudly against the metal ventilator. The most dreadful noise ever for a wake-up call. During the winter, our room could be very cold, and who wanted to get up out from under those covers? We had no heat upstairs. The only heat we had upstairs was the little heat that came through that one ventilator in the ceiling. And you'd actually be surprised that it actually made a difference. But it was not a comfortable warmth. It was still cold.

That next morning, I was faced with milking that cow. That was my daily routine every morning and every evening. It was my job. I remember very clearly after I had the cow in the stall that morning, ready for milking, and she was a-munchin on her grain, I stopped and smelled my hands to see if the perfume smell was still there. And it was. That sweet-smelling perfume was still very vivid on my hands, and oh, how I dreaded to milk that cow. I just knew after I'd be done milking, I would forever no more have that smell left on my hands. I sat down and started milking. After I was done milking, I smelled. I smelled again. And I was just sure that I could still slightly smell her perfume on my hands. I wasn't for sure if I actually smelled it or if it was a mind thing. I kept sniffing my hands numerous times that day, and I was just sure I could still slightly smell the perfume.

Isn't it just something what perfume can do to your mind? But I remember that as the best date we ever had. It was our first date together ever, and I thought she wore the best perfume one could ever wear, and to top it off, it even stuck to my hands. And I was really impressed how talkative and friendly she was to me. I also liked her laugh. I thought it was cute. I guess you can already see that this puzzle was coming right together for me, right? All that good stuff put together is what made this date so special for me. Perfume, friendly, and talkative. Now thirty-some years later, I would add coffee to that list, LOL.

Now some of you may have your thoughts as to how does it go anyway, to have a date with a girl and she sits on your lap for the entire dating period? You're sitting on a rocking chair in the living room with only a dimly lit light. Well, I am not ashamed to tell you, in all our three years of dating like this, Malinda and I never did anything out of the way inappropriately. We stayed morally clean the whole way through our dating period, and I am very pleased to be able to say that. I would *never* have dared to do or say anything inappropriately to her in fear of her being displeased and I would lose her as my girlfriend. Maybe even more than that, I would be afraid of it getting out to the whole church or all my friends finding out and humiliating me to no end. Even worse, I'd been afraid of my dad. I would definitely fit in with the story of *Mike and Ike: The Runaway Boys*. I would've had to run from home, because I'd been too afraid to face my dad and what he'd do to me. I just hated confrontations and still do to this very day. Hate confrontations.

If you never read the other book I wrote, *Mike and Ike: The Runaway Boys*, I encourage you to read it. I started out writing it because of my interest in hunting and trapping when I was a teenager at home. I patterned its beginning in the types of fears I faced as a teenager. My dad gave us boys some harsh whippings in our time as youngsters, and I'm not saying I didn't deserve some of them and I certainly do not want to condemn whippings, because the way this world is going with the younger generations and misbehaving, we still need this type of discipline in a bad way in our world today. Mike and Ike got themselves in a heap of trouble, and they ran far back into the mountains to live back there, thinking they would live happily ever after. And for three years, they did, but one morning when Mike got up, Ike was nowhere to be found. He was not in his bed. He was not outside. He was nowhere around. No trace of him anywhere. Mike lived back there for a couple more years by himself, thinking one day, Ike would surely, *surely* show up again, but when he didn't, Mike got so lonely back there by himself that one day, he packed up and decided to go back to face his parents and repent of all his wrong doings. He got this feeling that God allowed this all to take place because of his disobedience in running away from home. On his way out, still at the edge of the woods and with many days of traveling, he came up on this really old-looking house. It appeared that no one was living in there no more, so he decided to enter and maybe rest for a while. No other houses were in view anywhere nor had Mike seen any other person for several years since he and Ike had run away from home. As he walked up to the front porch which had been slightly caved in, he decided to first knock on the door, just in case, and as he did this, he was not prepared for what he saw. The doorknob turned. And life would never ever be the same for Mike ever again.

There was a time when my dad and I had a heated argument and I threatened to run away. My intentions were to run far back in the woods and live like the Indians did. I was sick and tired of this kind of life as it was and I wanted something else. But when I threatened to run back in the woods, my dad said, "Well, if you go and you get hungry, don't come home looking for food here." This scared me enough that I never did run from home, and I'm glad I didn't.

I'm sharing a little of the Mike and Ike story because of how different life's directions can go if one is not careful. *Mike and Ike: The Runaway Boys* is a 286-page book, currently in its second printing and still selling well. You will love the story. Information for this book is at the end of this book. Buy it and enjoy it.

I, too, was scared to make a wrong move and possibly get myself in all kinds of trouble with my dad. If you would ask anyone from the youth group that I ran around with, they would probably tell you that I was one of the wilder ones in the group, which would probably be true to some extent. What we considered wild back in the day would be considered boring to the young generation we have nowadays. But back then, we thought we were wild at heart.

Seriously!

But when it came to moral issues, I am happy to say that I never stepped over the boundaries there even once, that I'm aware of, during our dating years. Praise the Lord.

Now, I shared with you here that we dated for three years and saw each other only three times in those three years. I do want to clarify something here though. I visited her in Wisconsin twice, and she visited me once where I lived there in Ohio. This makes for three times. But during this one visit, I believe she spent like two weeks in the area visiting her married brother. While she was there, we had two dates during this time period. One was on a regular Sunday evening after the youth gathering and the other was during the week just before she left for her home in Wisconsin. In our area here, we were not really permitted to have dates during the week, only Sunday evenings, but we squeezed one in during the week with our parents' consent. I don't know that anyone else ever found out about it, and to my thinking, it was nobody's business, really. But then, when I went to see her in Wisconsin, I cannot remember that we had more than just the one date night while I visited. It was blizzardy, cold, and snowy when I got there. They had a dairy farm, and she got into her big old rubber gum boots and got right down and dirty with the chores. Oh, how I wish for pictures of those days. I was so shy and felt so out of place on this first visit that I am not really sure just how much I really enjoyed my time there during that visit. For one, it was blitzing cold. For two, I was meeting all her family for the first time ever, some of them. For three, I just wanted to crawl under the bed and hide somewhere. Yup, I felt very out of place. This was nothing like that first date we had earlier. Come to think of it, I wonder if it had something to do with her not wearing that good-smelling perfume this time round, LOL. Okay, I'm just kidding. I have no clue when I ever let her in on just how much I really liked her perfume that she wore that first time around. But we both laugh and talk about it now, and it made for wonderful memories for the both of us.

But you know what, looking back, there are so many things that I would do different now on a date than we did back then, that I think would make a date so much more fun and meaningful. For one, I just love going out to a restaurant to eat for a date night with her now. Going out for nothing more than coffee. Starbucks is a favorite of ours, although when it comes to the taste of plain coffee, Dunkin Donuts or McDonald's coffee beats the taste. Our purchase of Starbucks coffee is always a specialty coffee drink. Although with the direction Starbucks is going these days and what they support or stand for, sometimes, I wonder if it's time to boycott them. But I just love the smell you get from Starbucks when you open the door and walk in. Mmm, uhhh! Yup, that smell. That coffee smell, ummm, it's just wonderful. Coffee!

So for me today, I think going on a romantic date today would be to go out for maybe nothing more than coffee. Talk, laugh, and just have a wonderful time talking. Or going out to a Mexican restaurant to eat. We both love Mexican food. Sitting around on a couch where there are a few artificial trees or shrubs and maybe even a water fountain running. The sound of water. The lights on dim. Relax and enjoy the evening. Another thing I would do that we never did in our dating years is go for a walk together. Now thirty years later, I just love going for walks in the evenings. So I'm thinking how much more interesting it would be to go on a walk with your date. I would love that now. I think that would be so cool. But nope, all we ever did was sit on that rocking chair all night long and just visited. I was even too scared to ask for a drink of water during our date and my throat would be nearly dried up. The room we were in was warm, and on top of that, we were warm from holding each other in our arms all night, but I was too scared to ask for a drink of water. I just wasn't sure if it would be proper to ask for a drink of water and interrupt our dating time or not. Would it be inappropriate?

I guess I wasn't very educated on dating.

What would she think? I know we finally did go get us a drink a time or so, but oh, the nerve it took for me to ask her if that would be okay. We didn't waste no time off that rocking chair, and we were back at having our traditional date time again. I think back on these times now, and I wonder why we didn't try to be more creative on our date times. Of course, we only had a few dates in the three years we dated. But they were still dates. Those are times that I will never forget. Seems to me like even though we had to have our dates at our parents' house or relative, it would been so cool if we'd made ourselves some fresh coffee and sat around the table and drank that while we visited. But that was never heard of or I certainly hadn't heard of anyone doing it. I'm sure they do things a lot different nowadays than they did back in our dating years.

Growing up in my family home, going out to eat never happened. Only the very few times that it did happen was maybe the very few times I got to go with Dad to town during the summertime and we had to get us something at McDonald's for lunch. The closest town was probably nine miles away, so the option to go out to eat with your date, like the youth do nowadays, was not even an option. We lived far from town. Out in the sticks. And of course, on top of that, it was not permitted in our church rules. Now, thirty years later, I imagine some of those things may have changed or most certainly in a lot of church districts. At least I would hope so. Such man-made rules, my, my. Makes one wonder, how on earth?

Well, marriage came, and that's next. And the nerve it took to tell my parents, rrrr. Why does it have to be so hard?

Chapter 2

Marriage

A lot of water has gone under the bridge since those precious dating years. As I look back over my life now, a lot of those are memories I would not want to forget. But then, there are plenty that I would do much differently if I had a chance to do them over again. Malinda and I still enjoy talking and reminiscing of those bygone dating years. And our young bygone married years. How we did things before we had any children yet. It's funny how we sometimes lay in bed at night and some little thing reminds us of that first date we had and we start reminiscing about it and it still brings a warm fuzzy feeling within, just talking about those precious memories of our first date night. And that wonderful perfume she wore that night.

Have you ever had that happen to you?

Those are fun things to talk about, right?

Good times! Good memories!

In our letter-writing years, we must have hinted to each other about marriage somehow, but I don't know just how the question went about when I asked her about marriage. One thing I can tell you, it was not down on one knee in front of her and asking her if she would marry me. That I know for a fact. It was not about slipping a ring on her finger either. And of course, I wouldn't do that today neither. Maybe I'm still just too old school, but the Bible does talk about not wearing jewelry and God's word never changes. Men's ways and cultures do change, but God's word never changes. I choose to believe that it would be safer to obey and not wear them than to follow what most other people of the world choose to do.

And it was not going out on a special date anywhere outside of the home or going to a mall late at night either. "Would you marry me?" was simply asked in one of those letters she received from me. I'm sure it wasn't a shocker or even a real surprising question to her when I asked for marriage. We had been in this conversation in our letter writing about possibly getting married for a while, and so it was not a shocker to her. And so once we both sort of knew which month would work for us and we agreed on the time of the year, then I had to ask my parents about it, which was an extremely nerve-racking one. I did *not* know how to go about it. I was terrified. Embarrassed. I knew I would never have the nerve to say something to my dad first. The only other option was to go to my mom first. I dreaded this moment to no end. Oh, how I wished for some other way to make it known to my parents. I think Malinda even had to ask me several times in her letter whether I had already asked, and I still had not. But I knew it *had* to happen or we would *not* be getting married. Marriage wasn't just going to happen on its own. We were going to have to *make* it happen. I remember one morning after breakfast, after everybody else had already left the breakfast table and had done gone outside for the day, I finally mustered together enough courage and I got enough nerve together to talk to Mom. Yep, that's exactly what I did. I told her our plans. I didn't even ask her. I simply told her. I was too dumbfounded to ask her the question if it was all right if we got married. I simply told her we had plans to get married in October. Strange how some things must just happen, right? This was one of them. My mom looked at me with this half-approval and half–no approval grin on her face to where I was terribly ashamed and I could have crawled under the bed and turned into that little mouse just spying on the two standing there, Mom and I, had I known this would help me feel better. Right then and there, I could have run for the woods again and joined *Mike and Ike: The Runaway Boys* and never turned back. Yep, you're gonna have to read that story too, the Mike and Ike story. I wish I could remember her exact response, but what I remember was that she didn't think I was ready or maybe, in other words, matured enough to be getting married. I was three months' shy of turning twenty-one years old. You have to remember, I was the oldest of ten children and the first one in our family getting married, so this was going to go down a little hard to see their flock start taking off and flying the coop. Lucky me, LOL. I will admit, I was still young at heart, and I liked to try a little bit of anything, sometimes maybe things that seemed childish to my mother. Like the time I tried making a wooden scooter with wheels that I had taken off a wheelchair. These wheels were about the size of bicycle wheels, and it made for a really smooth ride. I had this thing all made out of wood, and it scooted right along. One afternoon, I was out there on the driveway in front of my dad's shop, playing with this thing when Mom thought I should have been working. Next to the road on our driveway was this little slope down, right at the end of our driveway, and so I'd get a little speed and coast down through there, right out on the road, and coast for a long time down the blacktop road. Mom made the comment that I was still childish and not ready to get married for a while yet. The fact of the matter was, this was before I had even let her know of our plans of getting married. In fact, it may have been before Malinda and I even made plans to get married.

But anyway, to get back to the moment when I told Mom about our plans, she said she would need to ask Dad about it. I said, "Are you telling me we can't decide when to get married?" I don't recall her exact words, but she did back off and said they would try to support us in it if there were no interfering plans in October. But somehow, somewhere along the line, we got married and we had a great wedding. I always thought wedding days were special. I always enjoyed going to weddings. The food. The songs sang in a wedding, those were special. The people and families that showed up. It was a big day. A special day. Ours was no different. My bride was special to me. She was now my wife. We got married in my hometown of Ohio. Her family, mostly from Wisconsin, all came for our big day. So not long after the wedding, we hired a big, long stock truck, used mainly for hauling livestock, and went all the way to Wisconsin to bring all of Malinda's possessions down to my area where we would be making our future home. We had made arrangements to rent a house about three miles or so from my folks and were overly excited to begin our future home there. Now some of you will notice that the wedding was at my house instead of at the bride's community. Let me explain. You're right. Any normal wedding would have been at the bride's home community. That would be normal for any Amish wedding. Ours was different for a reason, and it all had to do with my grandpa who was the bishop in my community. Grandpa never did like me much. The truth of the matter I believe was, he even liked Malinda's family less. Grandpa had a hard heart toward anyone who was slightly more liberal or advanced than how he saw things, and Malinda's parents had just recently moved to Loganville, Wisconsin, and Grandpa got word that this community might allow their members to use tractors for field work and you should have heard him boil. And you could probably even shower under that hot water, he was that hot. Only thing was we didn't shower. We bathed. What a life we had. In a case like this, Grandpa could have taken his two hands and wrung your neck soaking dry, because he thought he was right and you were wrong. He was a hard man. He did blacksmith work and fixed buggy wheels, but was never really good at it. Our wheels wobbled and rocked on our buggies. He raised a bunch of loose chickens in a chicken house and sold eggs galore. Grandma made homemade noodles and sold baked goods. I don't think they ever had much money and never did much traveling. I guess I make up for his traveling nowadays for what Grandpa didn't do; if you continue to read, you will find out. Today, we are a blessed family, and I give God all the honor and glory for His faithfulness to us.

I was not much for outside work such as carpentry work, as many Amish in our area did, but I loved to work with wood, building furniture, mostly outdoor furniture. This was a trade I had picked up working in my dad's lawn furniture business. After Malinda and I got married, I could work in my shop day in and day out and not get tired of the work. I knew long before I got married that this was what I was going to do if I ever got married. So this was a no-brainer. I was not going to be a dairyman. I was not going to be a farmer or a construction worker. I was going to build lawn furniture for a business and hunt and trap to my heart's content. Hunting and trapping were my hobbies. I loved it. Trapping for fox was my best hobby I think I ever had, next to actually raising domestic fox. Yep, I had found out from our neighbor that a fella in West Virginia was raising domestic fox, red fox, silver fox, albino fox, and others, and he would help me get started raising fox if I wanted to. I had never in my life heard of such a thing. I was on cloud nine if there ever was one. I was very excited to learn more about this adventure and I could hardly wait to get started. Surprisingly, my dad agreed to help me get started. Both my father and my mother knew that I just loved the outdoors and the woods and wildlife, hunting, fishing, and trapping. I often talked as a young lad, how I would enjoy owning and operating a zoo. A real zoo. I knew the exact spot in the woods where I could fix up a perfect location to have a zoo. But that would never happen and I knew it.

So one day, we hired a guy to take us to look at this domestic fox ranch, in mind to possibly buy some fox and get me started.

I was thoroughly impressed with the ranch. But the smell, whew, it stank. But I kind of liked the smell. You would have to be a true woodsman to like that smell. My dad ended up buying me two red females, two silver females, and one silver male. I was to pay Dad back once I made my money back from raising pups and selling the fur for profit. I don't know to this day if I ever was able to pay Dad back the money he had invested in these fox. Dads are supposed to be dads always, not? Especially to young kids who have no money of their own or a way to make any money yet. But in this case, these were to be my fox, and once they brought in any income, I was to pay him back. About the time I had gotten started was when Europe and some of the big fur buyers put this ban on buying fur from the trappers, and the fur market absolutely crashed. The animal-rights people were causing havoc to the real pioneers of this world. They are a bunch of people who needed a real life, instead of being out there destroying the real world. There simply was no money to be made in trapping or raising fox and expect to get rich off it. I had to come up with a different plan for these fox. I had a really neat little area fixed up in the woods down by the creek where I had set up my little fox ranch. The little worn path that I used to go from my dad's barn to the ranch was a little ways from our buildings. Overhead, between two trees, I had painted a sign on an old wooden board that read "Pink Feather Fur Farm." Pink Feather was an Indian name I had gotten sometime back when I read a story about Indians in a book and I liked the name.

The fur market had crashed so much that after I started raising fox, I never once skinned any of my fox to sell as fur. It was just not worth it anymore. So I had learned from somewhere that someone had started taming these little pup fox and selling them as pets. I got more information as to how you can tame a fox to be tame just like a puppy. I took the little pups away from their mother before they opened their eyes and I soaked this fox food, yep, regular fox food, looked much like dog food, and I soaked the food in milk until it was a mush and spoon-fed the little pups. I started selling them as pets, and they made the sweetest and friendliest little pets ever. I kept one as a pet up next to my dad's furniture business, tied to a chain just like you would a dog. This intrigued the customers so much, and this is how I sold all my little pet fox. I will never forget the thrill I got of raising these fox and how grateful I am still today to my dad for helping me get started in this business. It is something I could still enjoy yet today. This is one thing I am thankful to my dad for helping me with, and as long as I have a healthy mind to remember, one of my favorite childhood memories. My dad did not help me with many things like that. I was probably more afraid of my dad because of his harshness to me as a child growing up. I was the oldest of ten children, and it always felt like I got the hard end of the stick, so to speak. And like I mentioned earlier on, I was probably the one that needed the most spankings, I don't know. Why was I like this? Why? I don't need to question this anymore because I have come to the acceptance that God had a plan for my life all along, since he knew me before I was ever born, and I am forever grateful for this. I know I am where God has me planted right now. All in all, I feel like my dad and I got along pretty good, but when I couldn't meet the standards he thought were best, I felt frightened from him, and I would try to avoid him. At the age of being spanked yet, I would try to get to bed early and pretend I was solid asleep, so he wouldn't come spanking me. I would hope he would forget about it by morning or he would feel different about the situation. I think my dad tried to be the best dad he knew how, but looking back, I'm sure he too would do some things different if he could.

Chapter 3

The Fifteen Acres

So we got married on October 5, 1989, in my dad's little woodworking shop. About three months after we were married, we had all of Malinda's belongings moved to my home area there in Ohio.

The house we rented was right next to a shop where they also did some kind of woodworking as well. I think they had a contract with some kind of electric company making these large wooden spools to put heavy electric wire on. So I got permission to use this shop and paid according to the hours the motor ran. The shop was powered by some big old Wisconsin engine, and it had an hour meter on it. And of course, it was not an electric start engine either. To get it started, you had to crank it the old-fashioned way. About a year into renting here at this place, a fifteen-acre farm came up for sale, with a two-story house plus a food cellar and a large outdoor building with one end that had been used for a woodworking shop and the other end was used to keep the horses or cows in. This seemed like the perfect place for us. And the price, I thought, was unbeatable. It was just the perfect little place for us. This property was located on a gravel road which was probably the only downside I could see about this place. I was not fond of living on a dusty old gravel road. I still despise those dirty old gravel roads to this day. We have plenty of them around the Amish community right here in Daviess County, Indiana, where we currently live today.

The deal was made, and we bought the place. Talk about some newlyweds being excited. We had our own little property as young marrieds. A nice place at that. I started going from auction to auction and bought up used woodworking equipment for my own little woodworking shop. I have always enjoyed going to auctions, trying to find bargains. It wasn't real long, and I had my shop up and running. We had the perfect little place. We were still just young married, no children as of yet, although my wife was expecting our first child soon. How could life get any better than this, right?

Just how?

I'm here to tell you, life can seem to be going ever so good, but if you do not have the Lord Jesus in your heart, God cannot bless or prosper you with His blessings. Eventually, it will catch up with you. Eventually, it will, unless you repent. And as you keep reading here, you will soon see this happen in my life here. I'm not so much relating this story to entertain you but mostly to give you a clearer picture of what happens when you walk with God or when you walk away from God. Today, I don't keep focusing on my past, but I look forward to God's promises and my future as I serve Him.

The far end of this fifteen-acre place had a small patch of trees with a small ravine that started out on our property and ran over onto our neighbor's property behind us. I don't know where this ravine went from there. Could possibly have turned into a larger creek on farther down the line, who knows, maybe eventually out in a big river. But the really cool thing about this was, right out of those rocks in the side of this little ravine, out came a steady stream of fresh trickle of cold spring water. It was just a small slow, steady trickle of fresh spring water, cool as ever. There was no need for a well up by the house. The only bad part about this was how far I had to carry the water. I carried many a bucket of water from the far end of this fifteen acres all the way across the field to the house up front of this property. Sometimes, I would pull our little red wagon back there and get a couple buckets of water at a time so I wouldn't have to go back there so soon again. But imagine, just the two of us, Malinda and I, it didn't take much water. Most of my field here, I rented out to a neighbor, and he cut beautiful alfalfa hay off the field. That field raised the best alfalfa hay you could ever ask for. I was not much of a farmer myself. Wait, I already told you that earlier on, right? I'm not a farmer. So it made more sense to rent it out and let someone else take care of it. For every ten bales of hay, I got one bale of hay. That was more than enough to feed my horse.

Now as I write this book, thirty-some years later, I could just shudder at some of the things that I pulled off or put my wife through in our early years of marriage. I shared with you some of the best highlights of our dating. Getting married was another highlight. Beautiful to its fullest. But the part of the story that I'm about to share with you now is not only to shed light on some of my weaknesses but how frail a person can become. I thought I was a strong person and I would never stray.

The real reason I want to share this part of my story is because I now know how weak we all can become, and no doubt, a lot of people out there who are reading this part of my story can relate to either me or to my wife in some way. I dare not to dwell on my past because it could get the best of a person. I had to learn to forgive myself and totally trust in God, our Lord and Savior Jesus Christ, and let go of the past. I had to lift up my head, look forward to the future, and not dwell on the past. The past is the past. That's what that was, the past. I'm also going to tell you just how hard it was to let go of the past. This story is not easy to write about, and it hurts to the core. If I could just click my fingers and make my past be as it never had ever happened, I would. Many of us would. But you know what? There is someone who can do this. This is Jesus, and He tells us in Isaiah 43:25 KJB, "I, even I, am he that blotteth out thy transgressions for mine own sake, and will not remember thy sins."

Only God can do this.

Our first several months of marriage was a bliss. Good times. Fun times. I would live those days over anytime. We often stayed up late in the evenings playing checker games or there was another game we played with marbles and we just loved it. Young married. Just the two of us, Malinda and I. We often laughed and laughed and just simply were enjoying our young married life together. Back then, being Amish, we of course didn't have a camera. Now, looking back, I could just kick myself that we have no pictures of us at our young married life. How often I've wished to see what we looked like back then. What I would give for pictures of us in our younger years? Our first years of marriage. But those days are long gone now, and we have no way of going back now and paging through a photo album and reminiscing of our bygone days. Oh, how I wish we could. Precious memories.

Some of the Amish in the area were moving out and had started a new settlement in a new area over near Columbus, Ohio, due to the fact of simply not being able to get along with each other over here anymore. So sad. I believe the saying holds pretty well true to the fact that some Amish will start a new settlement faster than one can shake a finger at. All at once, they start to flock to this new area that seems good to them. And then just about that fast, someone claps their hands real loud and everyone flies like a flock of blackbirds. They flock in a new area like a flock of blackbirds, and they fly away like a flock of blackbirds. Never satisfied it seems. Most of the time, many are discontent. Some folks, it seems like, cannot get along with each other for very long periods of time or maybe they are just never satisfied wherever they are at. That seems to go for a majority of folks we grew up with. I understand not all communities are like this. But for a lot of them, this holds true, and I'm sure many of you can identify with me. Right during this time when families started moving out, a young English couple (non-Amish couple) bought one of the houses with a small portion of land off an Amish family who sold their land and then moved over to this new area near Columbus, Ohio. The county where these folks were moving into was called Pickaway County. Those of us who were not interested in moving out and felt like everybody should just try to work things out and stay settled where they were, we called them the Pickaway people. Sounded very fitting at the time. Pickaway County, Pickaway people, right? There was a lot of anger and bitterness between folks that were staying and those who were moving out. My mother finally told us boys to be nice and stop spreading the name Pickaway people, even though it seemed very fitting. Over time, things somewhat healed again because folks started coming around visiting again, and we, my wife and I, even went over there to visit a time or two.

This English couple just had a newborn baby girl and they needed a babysitter for the baby. Right next to where Malinda and I were living, sharing the same driveway, lived this Amish family whose shop I was using to make my lawn furniture. This was yet before we had bought our fifteen acres of land. They too were eventually going to move over to the Pickaway County settlement but had not yet done so. This Amish family had two teenage daughters who also became friends with this new English couple with this cute little baby girl who needed a babysitter. These two teenage neighbor girls started babysitting so the mother could go back to her day job that she previously had. This little baby was adorable. Cute little girl, with a head full of dark hair. Often, in the evenings, when the mother came to pick up this little girl, she had waited until her husband was home from work and they would both come together to pick up their little daughter. Since we lived in the little house right next to each other, we would also end up out by the car chitchatting with them. We all became good friends with this young English couple. They seemed like a couple that were in need of friends. For them to come around every evening and then hang out for a while became a habit, it seemed. Often, they would hang around just visiting and laughing, and they'd end up staying for a good part of the evening. Then there were times when the neighbor girls were not able to babysit due to their own work schedule that came in the way, and so Malinda started babysitting for the couple in those times. It came to the point that both Malinda and the neighbor girls almost fought to be the babysitter for this little one. Malinda really didn't have anything else going on, and it brought in a little side income for us. We really didn't have much of an income to begin with. We were only married for a couple of months, and basically, we had nothing. And so this babysitting thing got to the point of causing jealousy between the girls and us. We both loved the job, the neighbor girls and us. We loved this little baby. She had a head full of black hair and was adorable. We became very close friends with the young couple. We started feeling the tension between the girls and us because we both liked the attention we got from the baby and the young couple. Malinda and I knew there was a time coming when this family would be moving over to this new area near Columbus, Ohio, the Pickaway area, along with those that already had moved and others that were still going. This would then allow Malinda to take on the babysitting job without the tension it caused between us and the neighbor girls. And eventually, that's what happened. We ended up becoming best friends with this young couple. They lived within walking distance from us. In fact, we could see their house from ours. What happened then was they would end up having us down at their house for supper, and we would end up watching TV for a while until it was time to go home. They were aware this was not permitted by our Amish standards, but at the same time, they could tell that we were intrigued by the news or movies on TV that we were watching. Eventually, this became a real habit. We would end up renting movies and spending some real late nights at their house watching a movie. We enjoyed this for the most part, but there was also the part of where we didn't know how to say no whenever they asked us down for supper or just simply stop by to watch a movie. We were young. We were fragile. We craved the attention as a young married couple. We didn't know it at the time of course, but we had a lot of void areas in our life back then. We were Amish but did not have Jesus in our heart. We were following the traditions of men rather than God. We had no clue about the plan of salvation that Jesus had for us and that we so desperately needed. We thought we were doing the right thing by following the laws of the Amish. By the way, now thirty years later, I can verify there are Amish who know the real plan of salvation and they can live it while being Amish. But the name Amish will never get someone in heaven. The same goes for any religion. We all need to know Jesus and need to know we have accepted Him as our personal Lord and Savior. I didn't know this back then. The name Amish is what was most important to me, I thought.

There were times we really didn't have time to just goof off like this, but we did it anyway. The attention we got from them was something we longed for, just as much as they enjoyed the attention we gave them. In other words, we both had a void in our lives, and we were using each other to fill that void. They were not churchgoing people by no means. We were. But we had a big spiritual void in our lives and we were not even aware of it. We knew of Jesus but didn't know Jesus as our personal Savior. We didn't have that personal relationship with Jesus Christ. All I knew was we needed to follow the church rules and we would get to heaven. If we were able to completely follow the church rules, then there was a pretty good chance that we would make it to heaven. We had to dress *just* right. Our hair could not be too long but had to be *just* right with the church Ordnung. Well, I could go down a pretty long list of what it took to remain faithful to the Amish Ordnung in order to get to heaven, but it all remained just man-made church rules. By no means do I attempt to say *all* Amish churches are like that. Now years later, I have found a lot of Amish churches are a whole lot more spiritual than it used to be where we grew up. I understand some of these rules are needed to keep us in line from just doing anything our flesh so desires, but to hold to those rules in order to get us to heaven and remain in this church your entire life or you lose your salvation in Jesus Christ is living life in vain, my friends. In the Old Testament, the people had to follow the law that Moses gave the people. Jesus changed that when he gave his life on the cross. It is only through the blood of Jesus Christ that we can be forgiven and only our faith in him that gets us to heaven. Jesus said, "Come, follow me." Seek the Lord, and He will lead you in the way you should go. Don't run from God. Follow Him. If you truly feel God has called you to remain Amish and you feel you can live a victorious life living the Amish lifestyle, by all means, follow where God calls you to. Sometimes, God calls us out of our comfort zone into a strange land, but he will never ask us to do anything that would cause us to sin.

Remember, this is my story and our personal experience of where God has called us in life and told as best as I know how to describe. I don't plan to add to the truth or take away from the truth. Many of you will be able to relate with my story, I'm sure, because we are all made of the same stuff, all in need of a Savior, that Savior being Jesus Christ, and it's only through Him that we can be victorious.

I look back now, and I am just in awe of the road we had to go through in order for me to find the truth. To find my love for Christ. To find salvation in Jesus Christ. I was definitely a hard learner. Had to go through some real hard and very difficult situations before I opened my eyes to see the road I was headed down. It caused a whole lot of pain upon my family, and I look back now and wonder how God could be so gracious with me through all of this until I would open my eyes. It wasn't easy; in fact, it was pretty rough at times. Very rough. I'm just so thankful for the help I was able to receive even though it was years later. I had to humble myself to my lowest to admit myself into this program but have never regretted it afterward. It took Fresh Start Training Center in Daviess County, Indiana, a Mennonite-run facility with solid biblical teaching to help me understand how God looks at my sin.

If you are just like I was and you have a habit that you just can't seem to shake, and you know it is sin, but in the back of your mind, you always feel one of these times you will be able to stop doing what you're doing on your own strength. It won't happen. Okay! It just won't happen. Well, at least that's how it was for me. I would sin and then I would feel so terrible guilty and I would think, *All right, this was the last time I was doing it.* But then, as time went by and in a few days, that guilt had done passed away and that bad habit or desire had come back and was ever so strong again. So what do you do then? You give in just this one last time, once again, right? I thought I was strong enough to stop on my own, but I was not. See, this is exactly where Satan wants us in life. He will get you to think you're strong, and this way, he can keep you repeating the sin over and over again. That was my story, and I kid you not, I needed help. I needed someone to walk alongside of me and help me see how bad of a person I really was, even at the time I didn't think I was such a bad person. I had a bad habit that I did not know how to end. It would just keep coming back time and time again. At the time though, I thought I was no different than anybody else. Others are doing it, why can't I? But God was calling me out.

The truth of the matter I believe is, I am convinced that there will be many who read this book who can totally relate with what I went through and what I put my wife through. Today though, because of the help I was willing to receive, I can verify that my wife and I are deeper in love with each other than ever before. We are deeper in love today than we were back in our young married days, and we thought it was good then. But life threw us many curveballs that we did not see coming, but we praise the Lord for His faithfulness.

So back to the babysitting job and where this took us in life.

Chapter 4

Have I Strayed

So going back to the babysitting job. We became best friends with Larry and Tina, this young couple. Like I mentioned earlier, we would often go to their house for the evening and just hang out there. Either Malinda or Tina would fix supper at their house, and sometimes, we would simply go out to eat somewhere. And going out to eat was not a practice the Amish in our community did at all. Going out to eat only happened when we hired a driver to go to town to do shopping and we were in town most of the day. One thing about our little community was that the town where we did most of our shopping in favored our little Amish community by sending a little city bus out that made a route through our community every Friday morning and then returned that evening again. This was why we often spend all day in town. The bus picked us up in the morning and dropped us off in the evening. We did a lot of walking while in town. When I was still a young lad at home, it was a privilege to be able to go with my dad to town. For us children, it only happened about once or twice a year. We had to take turns. This was always a huge highlight for me. I don't know why, but I just *loved* going to town. This may seem strange to you, but I think today that I could probably live in town. For real. I always enjoyed seeing businesses, especially businesses that thrived to do well. Still do.

I'm gonna go on a little bunny trail here and then I will come back to the babysitting ordeal because this is the road that started us down the path to where we are today. What absolutely blows my mind though is the fact that God knew *everything* that was going to take place in our lives. Our future. We didn't. What blows my mind is why we needed to go down a valley of a very dark path first before we could see the light that was actually before us. The light that would one day bring us to Jesus Christ where we could repent of our sins and find freedom and peace in our lives. Our family. I did some very ungodly things in my life before I turned my life to Jesus Christ. I know I would not be where I am today if it was not for the grace of God and his mercy on my life personally. God truly worked a miracle in my life, and I want to tell you about it later on in this story. I want you to know that no matter how low down you might be in your life today or you feel like God no longer loves you or you feel you no longer matter to Him. I had to let go of those things that had me bound from moving on and becoming what I was meant to be. I needed to give my whole life to God, and I was far from that. I needed to let Jesus Christ be my Lord, and He would lead me on to greener pastures. That was a promise from God Himself. A Psalm from David: "The Lord is my shepherd, I shall not want. He maketh me to lie down in green pastures. He restoreth my soul, he leadeth me in the paths of righteousness for his name's sake." I am very thankful today for that provision Jesus provided for me and for you.

Okay, I got a little sidetracked there. Let's get back to the new friends we had made here. Our next-door neighbors.

Now that I was married and had a beautiful wife of my own, we also now had this young couple as our newly made friends to hang out with. We went to town much more often than your normal Amish family would and this young couple did it for us. Sometimes, we did it just to have something to do. Some evenings, we would drive far, often going to a large mall across the Ohio River to Parkersburg, West Virginia. It became a crazy bad habit. We didn't need a thing in town. It was just a fun way to kill time, blow the little money we had, and hang out with our new friends.

After this fifteen-acre farm came up for sale and we ended up purchasing it, we were now farther away from Larry and Tina's house, but that did not stop us from hanging out with each other. In fact, our hanging out with each other only increased. Matter of fact, the road we now lived on was a direct route to Larry's parents' house and so they traveled past our house a lot. Malinda kept on babysitting the little girl even after our move to this fifteen-acre place. It became a daily thing. Often, we even had the little girl over Sundays yet, and so we would dress her in Amish clothes and take her with us to church. A few months before we moved to this fifteen-acre farm, Malinda became with child herself. Now we too were expecting our first baby, and this was going to change our lives forever. I just loved and enjoyed to see the process of this first-time mom carrying a child, and it brings warmth to my heart when I think back on our young married life we had back then. Lots of fun, lots of good memories. Life was precious. But things would soon change.

As we moved everything over to our own place there at the fifteen acres, there was such a good feeling to have our own personal property that we could call our own. I immediately started building up my own lawn furniture business, making and selling lawn furniture, just like my dad had for about as long as I could remember. I do, in fact, remember when my father started up his business, but I don't remember much else before that, other than Dad raised a lot of hogs. Back in those days, little pigs were a good price, and Dad made a killing in the hog business.

Over on my fifteen-acre place, I made a home-made sign, nothing fancy, and I put it out by the road. Being we were sort of back off the main road, we did not have much traffic, and business was not taking off very fast for us. This fifteen-acre property was on a dirty gravel road. Dad's business was on a well-traveled road and was doing quite well. So he allowed me to help fill his orders in my personal shop and then take them over to his shop where the customers would then pick up the furniture. A downside of my business was I always got hindered in the evenings when Larry and Tina stopped by, and my work would come to a sudden halt because they would often hang around all evening. Sometimes, we would play cards at our house with them or hang out in my woodworking shop, and it hindered me from being able to finish my work. There were times where this really irritated me nonetheless, but then at the very same time, I really enjoyed their friendship. So it was as much us as it was them. I can't point fingers.

Our property payments were three hundred sixty dollars a month. We struggled tremendously to make the three-hundred-sixty-dollars-a-month property payment. There were months that we simply could not make the payment. We had no monthly electric bill to pay. There was no such thing as cell phones back in those days yet. Of course, even if there was, we couldn't have them anyways. And so we had no phone bills to pay. No water bills. No car payments. All we had to feed was the one horse and the dog we had and, of course, ourselves. That was it.

Were we really that poor or were we just that poor of stewards of our money? Our business? A lot of this simply boiled down to the fact that we just could not say no to our friends when we really should have. We'd run to town or go out to eat with them, despite not having the money to do it. We were best of friends; how can you tell your best friends no, right? It finally came to a point where we did tell them we had no money to go out to eat anymore, and they called us wimps. I guess they thought by us telling them we had no money was just a figure of speech. The fact was we were literally out of money. There were different times they would end up paying for our meals when we went out to eat, and this made us feel so stupid, but that didn't stop them from coming around nor kept us from going out with them to town. They needed friends, and we needed friends. We had this big void in our lives, but we kept looking in the wrong places to fill that void. We knew what we were doing was not going to work out in the long run. One time or another, we would ram our nose straight in a brick wall, and it was bound to happen. I always had this dream of becoming a huge furniture manufacture and have this big retail store, but the road we were on was never going to get us there. In fact, it was taking us nowhere near my dreams.

There were times when Tina had the day off, and she'd come over to our house during the day just to hang out and kill time. She'd done this many a times. But today was different. Tina ended up spending more time out in the shop with me than she did in the house with Malinda. I kind of enjoyed this, but at the same time, I felt really guilty when she did this. I knew Malinda was aware of it, and I knew she probably didn't like that Tina was doing this. I was married. She was married. I was a man. She was a woman. I was a churchgoing person. She wasn't. So in one way, it was safe, right, because I was going to church?

Wrong.

Now, Tina and I were not doing anything we shouldn't have up to this point. Just simply chit-chatting while I was trying to continue working on my project building lawn furniture. I would never have dared make any wrong first moves on her, even though I sort of felt like she would be okay with it. Tina was more or less just sitting around as I worked. She would get up now and then and walk around, tinkering around with my tools or whatever she got her hands on. At one time, she let me know that she wrote something somewhere in my shop and she wanted me to look for it. Well, I looked and I looked, but I could not for the life of me find what she might have wrote. But I got this warm fuzzy feeling about it. I kind of liked the attention she was giving me. But I never did find where she wrote something or what she wrote; neither do I know if she actually wrote something somewhere or if she just said this to see my reaction to it. I don't know this for sure, but I suppose she liked that I was searching all over my work bench and areas where she might have been, to find what she wrote. I suspected it might have been a flirting comment, and I was determined to find it. I never did find anything, but this led to her eventually giving me a real note and she told me to keep it a secret. This was enough for me to know it must be a little love note. I couldn't wait to read it. It was a little note, letting me know that she had a crush on me and she had ever since she knew me. Of course, I did not see this coming, never having had such an experience before and having no idea where this might all go yet. Like I mentioned earlier on, I feel like I was a pretty tame young boy while growing up through my teenage years, and even through our dating time, Malinda and I. Now, my mother and father might not agree with me on that. I don't know. But this is *my* story, and I'm telling it as I personally feel I experienced life and for you to understand all the things we, as a family, went through and where we are at today. I do remember I got my share of spankings at home. I might have been a little mischievous little boy during my school years, the things boys like to do, you know. Also, Malinda and I remained morally clean all through our three years of dating. In fact, I was pretty uneducated in these types of things (moral issues) until after we got married. But as time went on, Tina and I handed each other love notes about every time we got to see each other. This just kept the fire burning inside, and I loved the attention she gave me. I loved the feeling of it. In all of this, I had absolutely no intentions of running off with another lady ever and leave Malinda sit. That was the farthest thing of any of my plans. I don't remember even having a desire to leave. I loved Malinda, and I considered her to be my wife until death do we part. I was just enjoying the attention Tina was giving me. The longer this went on, the more relaxed I became with it, and I became immune to the fact that I can be married to Malinda and still play around with another lady. I knew that if Malinda would know about this, that it would hurt her to the core. I knew that. And so I knew I should *not* be doing it, but how do you stop something that felt so good?

Now if I may insert one little thing in here to inform you of the path I was headed down here, it would be this; again, I am not sharing this detailed story to entertain you with my life story, but much more to connect with those of you that may have had a very similar experience or may be going through this ordeal at this very, very moment. You'd like to break away from this terrible grip it's got you wrapped in and you just don't know how to break away from it. This is my goal: to share what worked for me, by the grace of God. That was the only way that I could do it. I always say that every one of us has a story to tell. Some good. Some bad. But we all have a story to tell. Share your testimony for what the good Lord has done for you. Your story just may help someone who has gone through exactly what you've gone through or maybe they are going through right now. They need to know there is hope. There is light at the end of the tunnel.

The real truth is, sin will take you much farther than you first planned on going, and it is *much* harder to get back out of it than it was to get into it.

We have probably all heard of the saying that goes like this: Sin will take you *farther* than you ever thought you'd go; it will *keep* you there *longer* than you ever intended to *stay*, and it will *cost* you more than you ever expected to *pay.*

The grip it has on you is tremendous vicious. It does not want you to let go. And then there was this one time that Malinda was away for the day. In fact, if I remember correctly, she had ridden the little city bus in to town for the day. Tina came over to the house, and I remember well when she offered me my first beer I ever had. I hesitated to taste it because I remember as a teenager growing up until I was married, I was pretty proud of myself that I had never ever tasted a beer. Up to this point, I was able to say that I'd never drank beer. This was a good feeling. Now, here I was being offered my very first taste of beer and even being coaxed to give in. I knew once I had that first swallow out of that tin can that I would never be able to say again that I had never tasted beer in my lifetime ever again.

Growing up, this was something that I had in the back of my mind that I wanted to hang on to, to never have a taste of beer. But at this very moment, I did let go of it. I tasted it. I would never again be able to say that I had never a tasted beer, ever. This saddened me.

Now that we were passing small love notes back and forth and had feelings for each other, how was I to say no to her? So I tasted it. With that first sip, I must say that, that stuff tasted nasty. I was not sure how anyone would ever be able to enjoy that stuff. But she coaxed me to just drink it slow and easy, and eventually, I would come to like it. Nobody likes the taste for the first time, she told me. I drank slowly, but I never did get the whole can down, and she allowed me to pitch the rest. I don't remember drinking much after that until sometime later again. We continued to do many runs to town in the evenings to kill time. Often, we did not need anything. You have to remember, this was back in the early 1990s. Gas was under a dollar a gallon. You could drive all over the place cheap. We'd walk around the mall all night, just killing time, and get us something to eat. This was where all our money was going. We would still always end up buying something, and this is why we were so broke. Couldn't even make our monthly mortgage payments anymore. We didn't make much money to start with, but it also didn't take much money to live off the land as it were.

As time went on, Tina and I did things that we never should have done. I confessed it to my wife, and I confessed it to Larry, her husband. But here is how this became about. Numbers 32:23, at the end of this verse, it says, and I quote, "And be sure your sins will find you out." How true. The young lady got so excited about the secret between me and her that she started talking to her coworkers about her involvement in all of this, and it leaked back to her husband, and one evening, he approached me about it. Well, being the dutchman that I was, I wasn't going to hide it from him, as it sounded like he already knew everything about it anyway. So I simply told him what happened. That very same evening, I also confessed it to Malinda, and you can only imagine how this tore her heart right out of her chest. This pretty much ended the relationship between us and this young couple as we had known it. There would be no more mall runs. No more evening runs to town for the fun of it. Although we did continue babysitting for a short time longer because Tina still continued with her day job and she had nobody to take care of her little girl. In the meantime, my folks talked to us about possibly building a new set of buildings next to them and sell our fifteen-acre property. This was to help us get away from the area where Larry and Tina traveled through every day. After much thought and debate (no, we didn't know to pray about such a situation back then), this seemed to be the most logical thing to do, and we sold our lovely little piece of property. I confessed my sin to the church and was faithfully forgiven by the church and restored back as a member. But deep in my heart, I was not a true repented person for more than one reason. I still did not see this to be as such a big deal. Everybody else was doing stuff like this or so I thought, and they can get by with it. God didn't strike them dead yet. The fact of the matter was I didn't see the real sin issue in all of this. The most devastating thing that I felt deep within was the hurt that I had caused my young wife. I hated myself for that. I had never really thought about the awfulness of this and how this could affect our marriage. I really didn't care about the church or any of the churchgoing folks; after all, I was still Amish just like they were, and this should get me to heaven. I really didn't care about anything else, as long as I remained faithful to being Amish. Deep down inside, I really didn't think it should even matter to anyone else. I had no intentions of leaving my wife for another woman, so this was out of the picture.

As time went on, we quit the babysitting job, and we went ahead and moved in our new shop that we had built next to my folk's place. We used one end of this building for our house and the other end I used for my woodworking shop. At this point, we totally severed our relationship with Larry and Tina. For a long time there, we had no idea what became of them. Somewhere through the grapevine, we had heard that Tina had gotten remarried to another fella. Larry also remarried, but we weren't in contact with either one.

Before we moved off the fifteen acres, some-where along this time, we had our first child, a cute but fragile little baby girl was born. Of all things, she looked a picture perfect to the little girl we had been babysitting for Larry and Tina. Even my family and some of our other friends thought so. It was abso-lutely amazing how much they looked alike. They simply could have passed as sisters. She had a head full of black hair. I've been told that a mother's eyes are what helps form or shape the baby, which I sup-pose could make sense. The person the mother sees all the time could have an effect of the baby being formed within because after all, it is directly tied in with the mother. It is how God designed a mother's body. It is uniquely made by the hands of God. I always liked the name Ruth, and so that is what we named our firstborn.

After we moved to the shop up there on my dad's place, about a year later, we had another little girl whom we named Miriam; this one was named after my sister. Today, she goes mostly by the name Mir, a short version of Miriam, a nickname she picked up from the youth she hung out with here in Daviess County, Indiana.

During our time living there in this shop just up the road from my folks, we had our third child, our first boy, named Lavern, and then later another boy named Marvin. Marvin was named after Malinda's brother, Marvin.

I continued making lawn furniture there at my shop and selling it right there, plus I helped my dad fill orders he had there at his shop. For the most part, I was never really busy, which I suppose was all right. If we had a booming business going there, it might have been hard to see the fact that the Lord had a different plan for us in Florida coming up, and of course, we were unaware of it at the time as well.

We sold our fifteen acres that we had over yonder to a young fella from town, the place I was so thrilled to have, was now gone for good. By this time, we were so far behind in making our property payments, I had lost track where we were at with payments. Being the loan was through Malinda's grandparents, it wasn't like a loan from the bank, and they might come take the property from us. By this time, it didn't even bother us to not be making payments. If we didn't have the money, no big deal.

I look back now and shudder at our attitude toward life. Today, I don't like debt. Our priority today is to get our debts paid off first. This makes life so much easier going, less worries, less stress, and less white hair.

Early on in our marriage, Malinda had another hard blow when we were moving stuff from the first house we had been renting over to the fifteen-acre property we had just bought. A neighbor to my dad's place came over to inform us that Malinda's younger brother, Eli, who lived in Wisconsin had just been killed in a farm accident. He was just a young teen-ager, not yet married. We quickly made arrangements and went for the funeral midway through moving. Malinda also lost her young brother, Marvin, at the age of only seven years old when he crossed the road to go see a longhorn cow that just had a little baby longhorn calf. As Marvin crossed the road, a car came flying over the hill and killed him. His older brother Ezra was with him when it happened. Ezra had not yet entered the road when Marvin got hit right there in front of him. This would have taken place in the Angola, Indiana, area.

Chapter 5

Back to the Homeplace

As time went on we were doing fairly well at this new location, just a quarter mile down the road from my folks' place, my home stomping grounds. We had a perfect view from each other, my dad's place and ours. My lawn furniture shop was nothing to brag about, but it was somewhat working out for me. It was what I loved to do. I loved to sell furniture and interact with customers. Making sales was a thrill for me. I enjoyed that very much. We had made our home at the one end of the building with just a plain old unpainted concrete floor with a small addition added onto the back which served as our bedroom. By now, we had three children. I don't even remember where they slept because we only had the one bedroom. In the middle of this building, we had our retail furniture store. Nothing fancy, just a plain old gray concrete floor. The walls and ceiling were not finished off at all, just bare 2 × 4 studs showing. I don't remember now if it was even insulated. At the far end of the building, toward the direction where we could see my parents' farm was then my wood-working shop. We had a nice little garden out behind the shop to the south. In the future, we thought we would eventually build us a house right here, but that never happened and I will explain why, here pretty soon, as you will see where our lives took a turn in a complete different direction and would never ever be the same again. But it was all for the good. Our lives went from bad to much better. But before it got better, we ended going back to our old ways of drinking and partying again, until that one day when both Malinda and I got a hold of ourselves and we wanted something better. Something where we would not be spending all our money as fast as it came in. We needed a change in our life. What we really needed was a change of heart. We had been living for ourselves up until this time. We knew nothing different. We were still Amish, and that's all that mattered. So we thought.

Spiritually, we had not gained anything by moving away from our fifteen-acre home we had over yonder. My relationship with Jesus had not changed anything by moving. I'd always been Amish, and I thought this was what kept me safe from eternal condemnation. The fact was this was probably about as far from the truth as one could get from being safe in the arms of Jesus. What I really needed was a real relationship with the Lord Jesus Christ and to truly repent of my past sins and believe Jesus could forgive me and set me free. To have a walk with Jesus Christ. To love Him with all of my heart, soul, and mind. That is hard to do when you have too many other interests in your life. I thought as long as I'm Amish, I was good. My haircut was right. I wore the right clothes. I wore black shoes, black socks. I kept my top shirt button closed; most of the time, I got scorched a couple times by the ministers for having the top button undone. I looked right. Went to church every other Sunday like I was supposed to. And I even held my tongue just right.

Now, before you walk away cross-eyed here, saying I'm condemning the Amish lifestyle, let me make something very clear here. This story is about me. I'm telling *my* story. This is my personal experience. These are the struggles that I personally faced in my younger years. I cannot speak for all Amish. I believe there are true Christian-living Amish today. Maybe a lot more so now then back in the times I was growing up. Back in my growing-up years, no one talked about spiritual things. It was just the Amish way or the highway. My grandpa was strictly Amish. He was nothing spiritual at all that I can ever recall, and he was the bishop, the shepherd of a church. And as far as I know, he died that way. Grandpa was a cold hard man. I knew him as a local farmer in his younger years, but in his older years, he worked as a black-smith, working with iron and he worked on buggy wheels, which would not last long on a buggy before it wobbled already. And I know there are still those types of churches around today yet. Maybe not as much as there used to be, but they are still around. Back where I came from, one could do so many things behind the church's back and no one would ever know. All except for one, and that was God. You could hide many things from the church. Or at least I did. And I know others did it too. But I thought as long as I was Amish, I was still going to heaven. Maybe it was just me that felt that way. I'm sure I cannot speak for everyone, but I'm going to take a pretty good shot here: some of you reading this right now know *exactly* what I am talking about.

So here we were, living on my dad's farm, hoping to get our lives in right order. Into that groove that felt just right and remain faithful to our Amish heritage. I thought that was what I needed to do. And I am very thankful for our heritage, but it needs to go farther than just that. We all need Jesus in our hearts.

It was nice and felt good to be able to walk up to my parents' place from where we lived and not always have to hitch up the horse and ride the buggy for six or seven miles each way as we did many times from that fifteen-acre place. I really liked my fifteen-acre place over there, but it was a long ride back and forth with the horse and buggy.

Now that we sold that place and moved over here, we would often put the little ones in the little red wagon and we'd walk up to my parents' place and just hang out there all evening. We did this often. It was my homeplace. It was a pretty laid-back lifestyle, and we enjoyed that part of it. But we were just living the Amish dream, that's all. My dream had always been to have a booming retail furniture store, crafts, and you name it. But at the rate we were going, it was never going to happen. We now had been at this new location for about three years already, and I don't think we'd seen Tina any time during these three years. But here out of the blue, one evening, she stopped by our new location and chatted for a few minutes just to see how we were doing. Before she left, she invited us over to her house for supper. She wanted us to meet her new husband. But there was more going on at her house than just to meet her new husband. They were having a huge birthday party for him, and she had invited a lot of their friends over as well, some of which we were acquainted with. We weren't in any stable part of our life spiritually at this point, and I don't think we ever would be because we thought just being Amish was what kept us saved. So there wasn't really any conviction there that told us not to go other than the fear of my parents finding out or the church and what they would think. Now they would look down on us again. Of course, we knew what they would think, and we really didn't care what they thought about it and so we decided to take her up on the offer. So off we go, why shouldn't we? This party turned out to be an all-out party. Loud music and lots of drinking. This got us right back out there partying and drinking again, and over time, it got to be an every-weekend thing. We were living it up. My dream for a huge retail furniture store was embedded deep within me, but at this rate, it was not going to happen. We blew our money as fast as we made it, maybe even faster, if there was such a thing. We kept our party times secret from the Amish church as much as we could, although I believe my parents knew something was going on. They probably knew more than they even told us, and it made us angry, especially whenever they confronted us about it. The whole thing probably wasn't handled as it should have been because we turned sour toward each other. I believe if our parents would rather have prayed for us and showed love toward us while we were in this struggle and had allowed us to see our own mistakes with time and let us run our nose in a brick wall or run ourselves flat to the ground, it would have been by far the best lesson that we could have ever learned out of this. This then is actually what happened later on which is where I feel the Lord was able to get hold of our soul and turn our lives around. By this time, the relationship between my parents and I had turned so sour that we had absolutely no interest in the Amish church anymore. I never did like confrontations, and the ones with my parents was probably the most unhealthy one of any. It caused us to part ways. We continued to party and barhopping every weekend, and we blew more of our hard-earned money.

We quit going to the Amish church, and so my folks told us we would need to move, that we couldn't continue living on their property if we were not going to be Amish. In the meantime, though, before we stopped going to church, somewhere along this time, my wife had started a job in town working at a sewing factory, and this was an absolute no-no. Working in town was considered extremely worldly to my grandpa. About this time, we were getting fed up in three or four different directions, including our friends we were hanging out with, partying, and again, blowing all our money, and we were getting tired of doing that as well. By this time, we were not feeling any love from any of my family at all. We needed to move because the building we were living in was technically still on my dad's property, so when they had asked us to move, we decided rather than cause any more problems, we would move. In fact, by this time, we *wanted* to move. As I look back on this situation, it just blows my mind how God works in mysterious ways. The valleys that God sometimes takes us through in order to make us stronger in the end is absolutely amazing. And then we have to stop, just look at the big picture, and think, *Is this what I had to go through in order to get to where I am today?* This is when I have to give God thanks for his great mercy and goodness on us, for all he has done for us. For the valleys he brought us through. It's absolutely amazing. It's mind boggling. But we praise the Lord.

So here I was, babysitting our three children while I was also working in my woodworking shop, and Malinda was working at the sewing factory in town. This was a much needed income, and it was bringing in a steady paycheck, not a real big one, but it was a steady paycheck, whereas my shop was not very dependable at all. While I was working in my shop on this one particular day, I remember it like it was just a couple days ago. I have no idea what in the world brought these thoughts to my mind other than God was moving in my spirit that day. We were seeking for something different in our lives. We weren't necessarily prayer warriors yet because we were just in the process of a real change in our lives, but God knew we were searching within. He knew our heart. But I just about couldn't wait until Malinda got home from work that evening to tell her what kind of inspirational thought I had just received today. Remember, this was in the year 1998, and cell phones were maybe just starting to come out, but they were in a big black case and looked more like a house phone but was plugged in your car cigarette lighter outlet instead. Cell phones were not the known thing yet, and we certainly didn't have one yet. So it was not like we know it today; you pull out that cell phone anytime you want and make that call. So bottom line, I couldn't call her. I was a little bit leery as to how she might respond to what I felt God was telling me we needed to do. I wasn't sure that she would like my brilliant idea, but I knew I was pretty excited about the thought I had received that day. So as soon as she got home, I immediately told her the exciting thought that came to me today. As she came in through the front door of the shop, I walked right over to her and I said, "Honey, you know what I was thinking today?" I had my eyes fixed directly on her to see her full reaction. "I think if you were okay with it, I would like to have an auction and sell everything we have and move to Florida."

She looked at me with this astonished look on her face, and she said, "I had been thinking the very same thing just today while working."

You should have seen both of our faces. Wow. I was almost in disbelief. How does this happen? Do things like this just happen, or was this a God thing?

Neither one of us had any such conversation prior to this, and as far as I can remember, we never even talked about this earlier on. Just suddenly, on this very day, we both had the same thoughts? I suppose for one thing, our minds and thoughts were both ready for a change in our lives. But Florida? Even more so, maybe God's spirit was moving within us. Back in the old days, God would tell people when they were to move. And where they were to move to. God never changes, right? He is still the same today, tomorrow, and forever.

That very evening, we did some more talking about the idea of moving. The more we talked, the more we knew this is what we needed to do. The very next day, I called up an auctioneer who I kind of liked because I attended different ones of his auctions from time to time, and I liked how they auctioneered, a father-and-son team. They immediately set up an appointment to come out and see what we had to put in the sale. They seemed to be impressed with what we had and we worked toward a date for the auction. The auction date just so happened to be on a Saturday when a visiting Amish minister was in the area and so the Amish had this same Saturday afternoon planned for a church service for this visiting minister. This wasn't a normal practice, but it did happen occasionally when a visiting minister showed up and he wasn't going to be around to preach on a Sunday, but the people desired to hear him preach, so they'd make church during the week. So they quickly got word throughout the community to all gather together that afternoon for a church service. The Amish in our area had no phone shacks set up like many of the communities nowadays have, so there was no way to get hold of anyone except someone traveled the whole community by horse and buggy and let each household know individually. The Amish church service was to be held at our neighbor's place just up the road that day, visible from our place. They were having church, and we were having an auction.

The day of our auction, we decided we would do the food concession as well and make a little bit of money from that as well. We had no clue if people would even show up for our auction or not. I questioned myself whether we would even have anything worthy to mention in the sale bill that was to be advertised in the local newspaper to draw a crowd. I mean, yes, we had some household items but probably more woodworking tools than anything else. I had some lumber piles, plus odds and ends. The auctioneers ran the sale bill in our local newspaper several times. Other than that, we didn't do any other kind of advertising. The morning of the auction, people started showing up, and I kid you not, we had people lined up along the road in both directions as far as we could see and beyond. We ended up with an unbelievable good large crowd far beyond what we ever expected. Things sold very well, and we even ran out of hot dogs long before the sale was over. So I talked to the younger auctioneer if it was worth my time to run in town to get more hot dogs or just forget about it. Well, it would be a little while yet before they were done with the sale, it might be worth going after more. So here I went to town, about an eleven-mile drive, after more hot dogs. The curvy hilly road made for twice the time that it should have taken me. I don't even remember then how many more hot dogs we sold or if it was worth my time to run after them. One time during the sale, the father of the auction-eers came to me and said, "The clerk has been keep-ing tab on the sale, and it's doing exceptionally well." Better than even they had expected.

Things were bringing a good price which would be much needed if these poor folks were going to start a brand-new chapter in their lives. What the future was going to hold for us was completely unknown to us at this point in time yet. We had no house lined up for us once we got to Florida. No job lined up either. Didn't even know a handful of people once we'd get there. We were simply doing this in a leap of faith, trusting God was going to provide for us.

That day was also a sad day for us. On the inside, Malinda and I both felt the assurance and leading to move to Florida, but we still wanted to question ourselves, are we doing the right thing? In a lot of ways, it hurt to be getting rid of all the things we had accumulated over the years, but on the other hand, there was no way we were going to move all this stuff to Florida with us. The morning of the sale, we were dead broke, totally depended on the next dollar to come from somewhere. Still, we had no worries. Currently, we had no electric bill to pay, no phone bill or water bill to pay. Not even a mortgage payment. I'm not even sure we had a checking account because we had no money to start a checking account. We were poor folks. The truth was, it should not be this way though. I had a furniture business. We should have had money in the bank and living quite well, but we were not. That's just simply not the case when you go blow every penny on partying every weekend. In reality, we had to sell our stuff in order to move. We really had no other option, if we were going to move to Florida. We had no money to have movers move all our stuff with us to Florida. We were headed south in hopes of getting a fresh new start in life. That *fresh start* would come yet, but certainly not in any shape or form as we had expected.

On the day of our sale, soon after lunchtime, the Amish buggies started going by our place one after the other. Everyone saw our auction going on, but not one of them would stop by. They were all headed to the neighbors to have church for the visiting minister. We were having the auction, getting ready to move to Florida.

Chapter 6

Moving to Florida

And so now, this starts a new chapter in this book, but even more so, a completely new chapter in our lives. This chapter in our lives would be a total transformation to everything we had ever known before. Now that we had our auction and pretty much sold all of my shop tools, we needed to make some fast moves to get out of here and get to Sarasota, Florida, quickly. Malinda had quit her daytime job at the sewing factory, and so all that we had to live off was the chunk of money we got from the auction, and so the longer we lingered around here, the more we would be using out of the auction funds. This fund needed to get us packed up, get us a rental trailer to pull behind our old two-tone gray Ford conversion van, and get us all the way to Sarasota, Florida. And no breakdowns along the way, *please*. We didn't need any extra expense to pay out as we traveled along the way. This van we had was a beauty in its own way, but old in another way. Talk about a beauty—it wasn't all that beautiful the very day I bought this thing though. The day I paid for this van and drove it off the lot, suddenly as I was going up this long gradual hill, this beauty simply shut down on me. Yup, the motor suddenly died right there on the road. Here I was out on a busy highway, barely off the road to let cars pass by. I sat there for a few minutes just staring at my dash and gauges, completely at loss of what to do. I was holding my breath, but my heart was still beating. What just happened? Maybe I even mumbled a bit to myself, I don't remember. I'm known to do that at times. Then it dawned on me: my van just died, what do I do? I knew little to nothing about these things yet. I opened the hood and checked the battery, but it was still good. The motor cranked over but would not fire. Being brand-new in the field of vehicles, I was thinking, *This could surely not just be happening to me. No, no, surely I did not just go buy me a piece of junk here? You have got to be kidding me.* And this was before cell phones were ever born yet. Calling for help would not have even entered my mind because there had never been such a thing yet at that time yet. So I walked up to the top of the hill to the first driveway to ask for help. Fortunately, lucky for me, I was in luck here. The old man was outside tinkering around with his lawn mower as I walked up.

"You sure you're not just out of gas?" he asked.

"No, I'm pretty sure of that. I just bought this thing about thirty minutes ago, and I filled the tank up with gas," I told him.

So he walked with me to the van. It didn't take him but a minute to reach under the dash and flip a switch. Then he said, "Try starting it."

I turned the key, and that thing fired right up.

"What did you do?" I asked.

"These older vans have two gas tanks, and the switch was flipped to the empty tank," he told me.

"Never heard the likes," I said.

Whew, what a relief for me. I thanked him after he wouldn't take any money. Of course, he didn't know how poor a fella he was actually dealing with right here either. I only had a few bucks to my name. I couldn't really count the auction money; that wouldn't be real fair. I scooted back into my seat behind the wheel again and went on home, feeling like quite the load had been lifted after that freaky little incident. For a little bit there, I thought I had just made a horrible purchase right there. And now, this van was going to be moving us to Florida, and it was going to need to run for many miles.

And so we didn't mess around much longer after the auction. We quickly searched for a rental trailer. I located a small U-Haul trailer, but we would never be able to fit all of our stuff in this trailer that we still had left over from the sale. There was still a fair amount of stuff that we did not want to sell in the auction, and it was never going to all fit into this small rental trailer. And then of course, the other problem we still had to deal with later on was where we would live once we got there. We hardly knew anybody in Florida to make contact with, and no one knew we were coming that way. The only people we really knew in Sarasota was Malinda had an Amish cousin living there, whom we hardly knew. Another couple that we got to know somewhat earlier on was Dan and Barbara Miller, known in Pinecraft as Plummer Dan. They were from Kalona, Iowa, and lived there during the summertime and wintered in Sarasota, Florida, during the winter. We did not even know how to get hold of them. Even if we did, I'm not sure they could've helped us out much. I had a great-uncle and a few cousins living in Sarasota, but never had enough contact with them to help us out either. So we were dead headed for Sarasota with absolutely no clue what we was going to do once we got there. We didn't even have a rental house lined up. I guess this is when you can say we took a leap of faith. A leap of faith that all would work out in its own way. Faith that God would provide for us. I definitely was not the type of person to sleep in motels. I thought this was the most ridiculous scam for taking your money. If we were to sleep *anywhere* other than in our van along the way down, it would be to stop off at some campground. This was back in the mid-1990s. Now twenty-some years later, I would see things quite differently. Not sure why, but I do. We never sleep in campgrounds when traveling nowadays. It's all motels. I guess things have changed. And we are not quite as poor as we were back then.

But getting back to all our stuff we still had, we needed a place to store it and then come after it some-time later on in life. Not knowing where we would be living at yet, we could not take the chance of moving everything with us just yet. So we asked our good old friend Warrior Coleman if he had a place in one of his buildings that we could store some of our stuff in till we can come back after it. He scratched his head and wiggled around for a while, but the good old kindhearted man that he was, he wanted to help us out. So he asked some of his married kids if anyone had some extra room somewhere. For me, it seemed like a rip-off to go somewhere and rent a storage unit and pay a monthly fee to keep our stuff in there for who knows how long. Before long, we would have more in rent fees than what our stuff was even worth, you know. That didn't make no sense to me at all. But lo and behold, had we just known everything, we would've been much better off selling a lot more of our stuff in the auction because as time went on, we had that stuff in storage for probably close to two years, and now we had absolutely no need for it in Florida. One of those items we had just recently bought before we decided to move was a brand-new wood-burning stove for heating the house. This was before we felt like God was calling us to move to Florida. I believe we paid close to five hundred bucks for that thing, and I was scared to put it in the sale for fear it would never bring what it was worth. The fact of the matter was, I think one of the Coleman boys ended up using it, and we never saw the first penny out of that stove. We got after them many times to pay us, but them guys outsmarted us. Most of the other stuff we had in storage we ended up leaving there as well. We had no need for it in Florida, and it was not worth the money to travel all the way back to Ohio to get it. We done had moved on in life. Some ridiculous poor choices we made along life's journey. Us poor Amish dudes didn't know much back then. We had just been living the Amish life, that's all.

We packed that little U-Haul trailer from the floor to the roof. The van was packed as tight as we could get it, and we needed to leave enough room yet for our four lively children somewhere in there to nestle down while we traveled. And here comes maybe even the worse part of this trip yet. This traveling to Florida would be our very first real road trip ever since purchasing our very own vehicle. We'd been all over town and on the back country roads here locally for a while already, but not out on the main interstates and highways with the speed limit up to seventy miles per hour. Nope, this was going to be much different. And to top that off yet, we were still pulling a small U-Haul trailer behind the van, which didn't help these poor new drivers out much. So then the day we planned to leave Ohio, the area where I grew up and knew as my home sweet home, ended up being evening by the time we finally got out of there on the main road. It got later then we had anticipated. By the time we got off our small local county roads and out on the main interstate, it was pitch-black dark. And I mean pitch-black dark. No moon was out shining to give us a little company for the night. And to top off all of this yet, this was going to be our very, *very* first real road trip ever.

Ever. Ooh, let me see here. I did mention that already here, didn't I? Our very first road trip like this, ever.

When I got that van up to the real speed limit out there on the interstate, it seemed like the road was absolutely just wheezing by us like we might be on a 747 jet, headed down a runway about to take liftoff. And I had never been on a plane yet either. Guess I didn't know much about the speed of a 747 jet either. I could only imagine. You have to remember, we had never experienced this before. This was our very first such road trip ever. Oh, I'm sorry.

Them rubber tires down beneath us were just a humming like none other. We drove all night long and made it safely to Sarasota sometime that next day. I don't even remember what time of the day we made it into Sarasota then. It took us much longer to get there than it should have. See, there were no GPS in those days yet or not to my knowledge. The big old road atlas was all we had to go by. For some reason, I guess I probably didn't understand the atlas just correctly because we somehow ended up traveling from Ohio way over along the East Coast and got down on I-4, east of Orlando, Florida, somewhere. We took the long way around to get there, but we made it safely, and we were one excited little family. We were right where we wanted to be, right here in Florida.

We knew of the Tourist Mennonite Church, and that was one of the first places we looked up when we got there. And as I mentioned earlier on, there was no such thing as cell phones. Well, I'll take that back partially I guess. The first cell phones that were just now coming out were those black phones in a black duffel bag attached to this long black telephone cord, like a coiled bungee cord, and it needed to be plugged into the car charger in order to work. It was by far not the handiest thing around, but it was far-fetched for this world back at that time. How in the world could this be possible, talking on this portable phone while going down the road? Not very many people had them yet, and it looked completely strange to see someone using one.

So of course, there were no smartphones either, and that meant there was also no googling or checking the road map on the phones or GPS to see how we were doing on time or if we were even on the right track. We couldn't google for the address or the location for the Tourist Mennonite Church or anything else. The Tourist Mennonite Church was about the only thing we knew of in Sarasota. We had no family around. Had no friends to stop by for a meal or to see if they might have any room for some visitors for the night. So we did about the only thing that was left to do: we slept in our van the first several nights right there in the Tourist Mennonite Church parking lot, pulling a U-Haul trailer behind the van wherever we went the first couple of days. Sometime later, we were told by some folks who had seen us or were watching us, they were very curious about this family with four young children and where they had come from or who they might be. They had been watching us, and every night, we would come back and sleep in the van at the parking lot. Mom, Dad, and the four young children. We also spent some time sitting in the van there during the day. There was nothing to do. Not for somebody that was new to the area and knew no one.

Looking back now, I have no clue how in the world we did it. Malinda and I slept in the front seats and the children in the back. It must have been one of the most uncomfortable places to sleep ever for us, but we were one happy family, we were in Florida. I was not about to go sleep in a motel. In fact, I doubt I even considered a motel back then.

One thing was for sure, we were in search for a better land. A land of milk and honey. Where would God lead us from here, we did not know, but we were trusting in him to guide us through this moment of time.

After about three nights sleeping in the van, we did find us a tiny little house. We named it "the teeny, tiny house." I don't know if I can put in words as to describe just how teeny, tiny this little house really was for a family of six. This house only had one bed-room. The bathroom was so small, you had to back in and walk out. True story. We used an old sofa that sat along one side of this creepy wall, faded of old white paint, for one bed, and I'm not sure where all the other little ones slept anymore. During the night, we kept hearing this loud creepy noise that had the rhythm sound of an old clock hiding somewhere in an empty house, and it made this lonely *ticktock*, *ticktock* sound. It was a bit scary. A bit creepy too, in this strange old, faded house. We were trying to sleep, but this creepy thing wouldn't let us sleep. The dumb thing was, we couldn't figure out where it was coming from or how to get it to shut up. We finally figured out it was coming from this old electric range cooking oven. I don't remember if we ever did get it to quit making that clicking sound then or not.

We lived in this teeny, tiny house on Bimini Street for three months until we finally found a larger house, just around the corner, next to the Amish Church on Hines Avenue and Estrada Street. Up until now, we were simply living off the money from the auction yet. Now that we lived here on Estrada Street, Malinda inquired about working at Yoder's Restaurant right around the corner from our house. Just a skip and a hop and she would be at work. In just a few short days after applying for a job, she was hired. This gave us hope for the future. Now we knew we would have a paycheck coming, and that was a good feeling. We would survive. Living in Sarasota was expensive. We knew that before we ever moved there, but we knew this is where we wanted to be, and somehow, it seemed that God had put it on both of our hearts to go there. Time would tell if we were to stay there or not.

It felt good to be this far away from the party life that had previously ruled our every being. Our money. Our lifestyle. Our family. The party life didn't give us hope. It only fulfilled our need for the moment.

I had in mind to start up my woodworking shop here in Sarasota as soon as I could find a place to set up shop. Woodworking was in my blood. I was determined to continue on with it. My dad taught me woodworking. This was what I grew up with. This was all I knew. As time went on here in Sarasota, nothing really seemed to fall in place as far as finding a shop to work out of. To rent something here in Sarasota seemed out of the roof, in my opinion. I wanted to do something from home rather than go work for someone else. So for starters, I sent off for one of these four- or five-foot-wide rug looms and started making woven rugs by hand. This went over pretty well, but it was never going to bring in the money we needed to buy us a house if we were ever to do that. The rent here was going to eat up more than this rug loom could ever fiddle out. I enjoyed making those rugs, but not *that* good. In the meantime, I would need to look for something that paid better than to fiddle with rugs. What Malinda was making at Yoder's was not going to get us anywhere very fast either. I had no clue what I wanted to do as a job besides my woodworking shop. I was not motivated to do work outside from my home. I didn't even know where I would apply for a job. After Malinda had been working for Yoder's for a while, she thought I should be the one holding an outside job, instead of her. So far, since we've been in Sarasota, I was the one that was babysitting our children while making these woven rugs. So Malinda and I talked about what would happen if I applied for a job at Yoder's and she would totally quit. Maybe this would open the doors for something better down the road for us, and she could be home with the children. This would make more sense, but oh, this was hard for me. Very hard. I didn't know what it was like to work for someone else. I really didn't want to know. The only other person I really ever worked for besides having my own business was working for my dad. I never held a regular job away from home working for someone else. Now, back when I was still a teenager, I worked at a sawmill that my dad had some shares in on which entitled us boys, my brothers and I, to work there. Not my favorite job either. In fact, if I was ever asked what was the worst job I ever had, I would have to say it was working at that sawmill. I absolutely hated it. Hard work. I found absolutely no joy in working at that sawmill. I was always very glad when something got messed up with the mill to where we couldn't saw logs. Dull blade. Engine quit running for some odd reason. Anything. And that did happen. For me, as a young boy, that was a good day.

Chapter 7

Humbly Doing My Job

Back to finding my job in Florida. I really wrestled with this thought as Malinda and I discussed the possibility of it coming to that yet. She was away from home every day, and I was at home taking care of our children. I wanted my own business. Nothing else. That's all I wanted, to have my own business.

Reluctantly, I gave in, and I applied for a job at Yoder's restaurant. This would have to do for the time being. I don't know how well I slept that night. Working in a restaurant was going to be far different than anything I'd ever done before. That very next day after I had applied for a job, I got a phone call from the restaurant, saying I got the job. I was going to start out as a dishwasher. Go figure, huh? Wash dishes? Unbelievable. Oh well, it wasn't washing dishes quite like I was used to seeing my mother wash dishes at home. I would be working with an automatic dishwasher. Either way, it didn't sound very appealing to me. Lo and behold, I had not much more then received that phone call of having been given the job, when that very same evening as I was walking through Pinecraft Park watching the youth play volleyball, when a well-groomed gentleman walked up to me, grin on his face, like maybe I was supposed to know him as he tried to start a conversation with me. Didn't take me long to figure out he was from Sunnyside Mennonite Church, the church we had just recently started attending. I knew a few people from there just by recognizing their faces, that's about all. We had not been attending there long enough yet to where I knew many people yet. He introduced himself as Bill Yoder. We made some small talk and then he asked me if I had a job yet or if I was still looking for something. He'd heard earlier that I might be looking for a job. Then he told me what he had in mind. He was in the process of purchasing this business that operated forty thousand laying hens, located just east of Sarasota. About six miles east from Pinecraft. The minute he shared that with me, I about flipped. My stomach did a flip-flop. I told him how I had just applied at Yoder's the day before, and I just got the phone call today, and they want me to come in to work first thing Monday morning to start as my first day. I could have just kicked myself about right then. So what do I do now? Go back and tell them that I got a better job offer *before* I ever get my first day put in with them? Yikes.

Butterflies were swimming all through my stomach, some nearly came up my throat.

Well, I am actually in the very early stages of buying the farm, he told me. The way it looked, I would be buying it, but until then, he suggested I go on with my job at Yoder's Restaurant for the time being because I wouldn't be able to start right away anyway. Not until he bought the business.

There was light at the end of the tunnel. This gave me some really high hopes for the future. The Lord had brought us to Florida, and now he was providing a good job for me. Maybe even better than I could have imagined. This felt like something I would actually enjoy as a job, and we could survive here in Florida. Nevertheless, I will be forever grateful to Almighty God in how this all took place because looking back now, I can see how this paved the road to our future for our entire family. Even though today, while writing this story, we now live in a total different state and I'm in a total different business. Today, I'm in a total different business then I ever thought would be possible. The road was being paved already years earlier. God knew our future, and he was paving the road ahead of us. It just blows my mind sometimes, when I look back at the road I had to travel through to get to where I am at today. This is in relationship with my business and my relationship with Jesus Christ and my family. Along this journey, there are many things that I would change and do differently if I could do my life over. Many of my failures in life are things I picked up after we were married, and I think this is so sad to say, and it's embarrassing, but it's true. I can't change my past, but I can change my future as I strive to live for Christ. Often, when someone's life gets all messed up, you look back and say, "Well, it's easy to see why he or she turned out this way because of his or her upbringing." But that's not necessarily true in my case. This all came about from the pure pressure, hanging out with wrong friends in our early years in our married life. It was still the choices we had made. Now looking back, I can see God's hand guiding me all along the way, despite the sin that so heavily weighed me down in my earlier years. God knew the road I would go down and that there was going to be a time in my life that I was going to repent and I was going to come back to serve Him again. God knew that. He knew that all along. God knows our future; otherwise, I suppose He would have given up on me and you a long time ago already. It's just absolutely amazing if you stop and think about it. If it was not for the job I took on at Sutter's, this chicken farm with Bill Yoder, the road it paved for my future would surely be different today as well.

Working at the restaurant was a good experience for me, and I did enjoy my job for the most part. I got to make a lot of new friends while working there and am glad I had the opportunity to work there.

While working at Yoder's Restaurant, Bill Yoder kept me informed as to how the process was going with the purchase of the chicken farm. There were times I thought it was taking a long time, and

I started wondering if it was ever going to happen. The day came when Bill told me that I could start my new job at Sutter's in January of 1998. He would not be taking over the chicken farm until March of that year, but he wanted me to get started so that I could get a head start in training under the old management and get to understand everything that is involved there with the farm. I would end up being his right-hand man there on the farm, as Bill would say, given the title "farm manager," taking care of the chickens, gathering the eggs twice a day. Keeping the manure hauled off. The manure was hauled to this hippie farm where organic produce was grown and sold to dealers everywhere. Some of the nicest, richest-looking produce you ever laid your eyes on. The owner here was a real hippie. You didn't cross his path the wrong way, and I quickly learned to dump the load of manure where he told me to or else get a good chewing out. And I don't ever remember seeing him in shoes. He was always barefoot. That rich black soil poked up between his already dirty toes as he would march out to meet me with every load I delivered. That rich black soil was powder fine, totally mixed in with this rich chicken poop I delivered to him. You can only imagine what his bedsheets might have looked like. Oh, I'm guessing he took a shower every evening, but still, day after day, can you imagine the dirt-stained feet that met up with clean white sheets. Not only that, you should have seen his employees. Yep, same thing. Ladies and gentlemen, all alike, all in the same boat. Nonetheless, it was an experience

I will not soon forget. Not to mention this one time that I was pulling up through the field headed back out toward the road with plans of going after another load. As I sometimes needed to do, I'd need to go through his drive-through shed to get to this one particular spot to dump out back there. As I was pulling up to the shed, I hear this horrendous scream coming from the top of this hippie's lungs. I think all valves were wide open on his lungs that time around. I quickly stopped, only inches away from pulling into this shed with my dump still way up in the air. I'd forgotten to let my dump bed down on my truck. You talk about a near heart attack. I don't know which was closer to giving me a heart attack, the thought of what if I hit his building or the horrible damage I'd done to the dump truck had I hit. The thought of this hippie's mad attack on me. I can only imagine. Dirt flying some twenty feet up in the air from his bare feet and more horrendous angry screams. Would not have been pretty. Memories! Memories of what I would call fun times, hard times, and near-heart-attack times.

While I worked at Sutter's, I can honestly say I tried to do my job as though it was my own business. I did my best. I wanted to please my boss. My boss was not just my boss, he was also like my best friend. For the first several years, things seemed to go very well in that way. I am not sure what happened, but toward the last part, after four years with the farm, there were things that were not working out as well and I got really burned out and I totally lost my interest in the farm. This was gut-wrenching for me. I was struggling tremendously with the good memories and close relationship I had with my boss, Bill Yoder, in these past four years. Now it seemed we were at a fallout, and I was losing that good relationship I once had with my boss. Things were suddenly not the same there for me. I didn't know what else I would do for work, but I could feel deep within my heart that it was time I started thinking about something else for my future. I felt this job slipping from my hands as each day passed. With other employees on the farm, but not necessarily interfering with my personal job title that I had, it seemed I somehow became jealous and felt like they got most of the boss's attention and my part in the business didn't matter that much no more. At least that is what I was feeling. It was a horrible feeling. This was probably not the case at all, but things like this have a way of getting to you when you see another employee getting a lot more attention. If I could have seen through all of this, possibly this individual needed more attention on a specific work area on his job than I did on my end. But I was there first, I thought. I was his first hired employee after he took over. I had the right to have the most attention, right? That's what I was feeling. It came to the point where I didn't even want to talk to my boss anymore. I was becoming angry. I was hating my job, and I wanted out. At the same time, I didn't want out. I battled with this for some time. I don't even remember taking this to the Lord in prayer. I wasn't a man of constant prayer. I was frustrated, and I was trying to work this out on my own, and I figured it would all come out okay at the end, I guess. Well, eventually, it did. But again, like so many times before, it certainly did not come out like I would ever have imagined. Somewhere along the way, my boss and I must have talked through some of my frustrations, and it came right at a time when Bill already had some other ideas rolling around with the business. Bill figured out buying eggs from other farmers and getting them trucked in was making him just as much money or more as having his own farm. Buying feed by the semi-load, paying me full time to run the farm, paying all the other employees who came in three days a week to help in the grading process, it made sense to look into doing something different. There was a lot of hard work and other things that went into producing these eggs, and at the end, the finished product was twelve eggs to a carton, one egg at a time, filling case after case. Looking at all the overhead expense that went into this operation, it made sense to sell off the chickens and go all the way into buying all our eggs from other farmers who were a lot bigger operators than what we were with forty thousand laying hens. So one day, Bill asked me if we could go out for lunch. We went to this little place called Wings and Winnies, a little hole-in-the-wall restaurant. If you liked hot wings, this was definitely the right place for you. I never was much of a hot food eater, but wings is one of my favorite meats from the chicken. I could never understand why you'd eat something so spicy that you'd take one bite of chicken and one gulp of water, one bite of chicken and another gulp of water. Maybe you need to call that a hot watered-down chicken.

I always did enjoy going out for lunch with Bill because I never knew just what he might have up his sleeve this time. And this time, it was different. We needed to know how we were going to move away from the chicken business. If we were to get rid of the chickens, we needed somewhere to go with forty thousand laying hens. That was a lot of chickens to get rid of. During our visit, I took it upon myself to get rid of all the chickens. Bill said he'd pay me a percentage per hen if I found a way to get rid of them all. I wasn't exactly sure how I was going to get rid of forty thousand hens just yet, but I had some good ideas and I was excited to take on this challenge. I started off by cutting cages apart and filling them with about a hundred hens per week and taking them to this small animal auction out in Arcadia, Florida, about a forty-five minute drive from Sarasota. The auction was held every Friday evening and often went late into the night before everything was sold. Often, I didn't get home until midnight. But by the time the next Friday evening came around, I was ready to go again. I'd sell more chickens. I took chicken crate after chicken crate to the sale till I nearly flooded the market. The main buyers were taking notice of me coming in every week with these same type of chickens week after week.

Bill gave me a time limit as to when I needed to have all the chickens out of the building. One of those reason was the feed supply. The longer we still had chickens in the houses, we needed to buy feed. Ideally, taking twenty hens to the sale per week would kept the market price up there and would not have flooded the market. But I had a time frame I needed to work with. So I started taking chickens out one hundred at a time. It wasn't very long until some of these buyers figured out someone was going out of the chicken business and the prices started coming down dramatically. Would not be really long and it was not going to be worth my time running out there every week. After several weeks into this, some muscular fella with scroungy-looking facial hair approached me while I was standing around watching small animals sell. All I wanted was for my chickens to sell so I could go home.

"How many more of these chickens you got?" he asked.

It didn't take a rocket scientist to figure out that these same-looking white laying hens are coming through the sale every week and always in these same style of wire cages. See, I was cutting the wire hanging cages apart piece by piece, filling them with chickens and then I was also selling the cages after the hens were sold. But this fella caught me off guard when he asked me this question. I wasn't sure how I wanted to answer him. If I told him I got thousands to bring in yet, he would definitely not run the price up no more at the sale, because he knew eventually, the price was going to drop. He was one of the big chicken buyers at this sale, and he was there every week to buy. He was one of those guys that would buy up these chickens and take them back down to Miami, Florida, and sell them to the Mexicans or Cubans down there. Some of these buyers paid good prices for these chickens. See, I was not the only person bringing in chickens. There were hundreds of other chickens there as well. From the fancy show type of chickens to downright good eating chickens. Some of these buyers ran the price way up there just to outdo the other buyers. I don't know how they made all their money back on some of the prices they paid. Starting out, I did really well on the chickens, but then the price got so low that I wasn't sure it was being worth my time anymore.

So how do I answer this fella? I stuttered around there, trying to hear him out. I wanted to see where he was going with this. But he was standing tall right there in front of my face and right up blunt with me. He straight out asked if I had hundreds more, and if I did, he wanted to know if he could come directly to the farm and buy them directly from me instead of having to go through the auction barn. My mind went spinning a hundred miles an hour. Do I kind of blow it off as yes, we may bring out several more, not sure, all depends? Or do I straight out tell him what we got left out there, possibly sell the rest of the flock to him? Back of my mind, I was thinking as long as I keep bringing them out to the sale barn like this and buyers keep running the price up, I could make a lot more money. But if I flood the market, then the price will drop and it'll bring the price of all the chickens down, including the fancy show chickens. I didn't want that either. So I told the fella that I had about thirty-five thousand hens left yet. He didn't stutter a word; he simply asked, "Can I come take a look at them?"

I was shocked at his response. Could hardly believe I may actually have someone interested in the whole flock. I wasn't sure whether to be excited about it or if I did a stupid thing by giving him the address of the chicken farm. Would I regret doing this? Now he knew where these chickens were coming from. No more a secret and no more paying the auction price.

The next day, I said something to Bill about it. After discussing with him a bit, we decided this would be the right thing to do. We just wanted to get rid of the birds, whatever it took. I don't think either one of us was sure if we'd ever see the fella though. Lo and behold, he showed up, and he even had his wife with him. Instead of paying for the whole flock of thirty-five thousand that we had left, he wanted to pay in segments. I think thirty-five thousand hens looked a little overwhelming to him. This was going to be a lot of chicken to butcher. They hauled chicken after chicken after chicken out of there until I imagine they were seeing chicken in their sleep. After numerous trips out to the farm, they got slower and slower and slower at pulling hens from the cages and then they'd miss a day here and there and then they'd miss several more days in between a load, and all at once, they didn't show up anymore at all. Later on, thinking about this deal, we should have stuck to our guns and tried having him pay for the whole flock before we made the deal so that he had to take them all.

I called him again and again, but when he finally did answer, he told me they just can't seem to get rid of them anymore. I guess wherever they were taking them, they were flooding the market as well. Rumor had it that many of these buyers were taking these chickens to their families in Miami, Florida, where the Cubans gathered by the thousands and they'd butcher them and send them over across the water to their poor families over yonder.

Hmmm, well, now what?

I still had over half the chickens left. *Half of them*. I needed to get rid of them somehow. We were no longer processing the eggs, but we were still needing to keep feed in front of these chickens as long as we still had them. The water still needed to run through the lines. The lights still came on throughout the chicken houses. It took the electric motors to run the feed conveyors to take feed from one end of the buildings to the other. This still brought about a large electric bill that had to be paid. It was time to put an end to this part of the business.

I took more chickens to the auction, but the price had dropped so low, it was not worth my time back out there no more. I was scratching my head as to what to do next.

Sleep!
Think!
Sleep!

Think!

Got another idea.

Then I remembered someone else. We had an older fella, a foreign guy as well, a pretty feeble guy, but still seemed to be getting around fairly well for his age that every now and then came out and bought chickens from us off and on. I don't know what he did with the chickens, but it could not hurt to give him a call. So I called him up. Yup, by now, cell phones had come in. My first carry-around cell phone was pretty clumsy, big, but I loved it. I told him we had about twenty thousand laying hens left in our house, and we were looking to get rid of them all. I would give him a really good deal on them. It didn't take him no time to come out and take a look at what we had. I shot him a price for taking them all. Lo and behold, he took me up on the price. He made trip after trip with loads of chickens, but he too got really, really slow there toward the end. Finally, toward the end there, I started hauling them over to his farm myself just to get them chickens out of our barns. Bill, my boss, had informed me that he did not want to buy another load of feed once the current bin of feed was empty. At last, I got rid of them all. No more chickens.

That was the end of the chicken farm as we knew it. And that farm right there would never be the same ever again. And no more hauling chicken poop to the hippie farm either. This part of the business was over.

Chapter 8

Selling Produce

I worked at Sutter's Egg Farm for approximately five years. This was half of all our time we lived in Sarasota, Florida. The farm was making big changes, but I continued to work for Bill on the farm for just a little while longer yet. At the same time, I was also trying to come up with something I could go out on my own on. We've been in Florida long enough now that I was ready to venture out there on my own. We now lived here long enough to understand Florida, and it felt like home to us. Florida is expensive. It's warm. It's beautiful. The fresh aroma of citrus blooms in the air most of the time, umm, just something about it. The palm trees bring that beautiful warm feeling within somehow, not sure I can put in words the feeling. It's home. To us, it was home. Florida is not for everybody, but to us, it was.

I was ready for my own business. I didn't want to go looking for another job working for someone else.

I had a couple of ideas running through my head. Both ideas should work out pretty good, I figured. Both should make pretty good money. As I mentioned earlier on, one of those jobs was more on the dirty side. That was getting into a lawn-mowing business. Dirty, as in dusty, dry grass as ya mowed grass on sandy soil here in Florida. Every other neighbor had a lawn-mowing business here in Sarasota. Well, that is not exactly true, but almost. There were a lot of them around. And there were several lawn-mowing businesses that were for sale. I could see myself doing something like this, I thought.

I knew it would be a very warm job in the summer, but that's why I liked Florida.

It was warm.

And dirty.

I didn't care a bit for the cold. I'd rather had the Florida warmth.

Dry grass makes for some nasty dust in the summer.

But I always thought it seemed like those lawn-business guys had a lot of money. And yes, I understand, it's not all about money. But I always admired someone who could manage a business that prospered and did well. And a lawn-mowing business in Sarasota seemed like a prosperous business to me.

The other business I thought about going into was selling fresh grown Florida produce on the retail end of the business. My wife had worked at Detweiler's Produce when they first started out at Sutter's, under that little roof out front where we sold eggs to local customers for years. For a little while there, Henry Detweiler and his children also helped in the egg-grading room where I worked a couple days a week, besides my regular job back out there on the farm. Then for a little side job, Henry started selling some produce out front. He would run to Plant City, Florida, to this large outdoor wholesale produce market with his pickup truck and load it as full as he could get it without it falling off the side of his truck. Most of the produce was raised locally right there in Plant City area, during the growing season. Produce was brought in to Plant City from other places when it was out of season right there in Florida. Fruits and vegetables would start coming in from other states. The best peaches always came in from Georgia. The best strawberries ever were raised right there in Florida. No joke!

This produce thing for Henry soon outgrew the small area out front under that little roof. So Henry looked for another place to sell his produce. Another location, only a few miles up the road, out on Fruitville Road was soon rented. Lots more space. Lots of room to grow. After Henry moved the produce business out to Fruitville Road, Malinda didn't work as much for Henry anymore, and eventually, she totally quit. This was the best thing Henry could have done though, to move to a larger spaced area. From there, it became Detweiler's Produce, and the business absolutely boomed for him. This was right on the main stretch of a busy road, and it didn't take long for people to find out about this place. But eventually, Henry found himself in another snare. The owners of this place Henry was renting from now wanted that building back and use it for their own business selling produce. They actually had an orange grove right there on the farm and sold their oranges right there as well, but after seeing what the other produce did for Henry, they decided they wanted to do this for themselves. So Henry had to look for something else again, which proved again to be just the right move for them. The location was good, but the building probably wasn't as large as what he just moved from, but his customers followed him right over to the new place. The place he had just left behind never could do business as the Detweiler's did. Customer service, friendly faces mean more then location, often.

But while Malinda was still working for Detweiler's over at the Sutter's location, I also helped a little here and there as time allowed, but mostly, I was still on the chicken end of the farm; nonetheless, I had my eyes and ears wide open all this time, taking in any lessons I could learn. At this time though, I don't remember I ever thought that one time, I might get into the produce business myself. But if you remember, like I said before, I've always admired businesses who prospered and did well. Having grown up in my dad's woodworking shop and then getting married and having my own shop, I have always been all ears to learn how others did it. All eyes and all ears. I loved reading success stories wherever success stories were written, whether in a book, magazine, or newspaper. I read and reread Sam Walton's book, the founder of Walmart. That book was probably one of the best success stories I ever enjoyed reading, and then later on now, the founder of Pilot truck stops, that was a very interesting book as well. That guy right there was a pretty down-to-earth kind of fella, and he grew into a huge business selling fuel along major interstates. After reading his book, it was almost like I had gotten to know the guy. He didn't allow his mistakes to get him down, but in fact, he learned from his mistakes and prospered from them. Now, most of us traveling on the interstates, we stop in at his truck stops, the Pilot truck stops. Interesting book he wrote. No, I have absolutely no interest in selling fuel and probably never will, but the lessons he shared with his business were very encouraging and valuable to me. It was a true story of success.

I was pretty confident that I could do well if I decided to go into selling produce on the retail end of the business. I took notice how people loved to buy fresh produce. I was watching. I was listening. It was a fast turnaround on your money. Fresh produce sold right now. The only thing that probably bothered me the most was that I was not going to be opening up anything close by our home area though because Detweiler's was already there. So I would need to go out of the area a bit. That was still not the biggest thing holding me back though, if anything was. I still did not have a lot of money to get started with. No, we were no longer these poor, poor folks like we once were, but we had other bills to pay now. Getting into a full line of produce could end up being a pretty hefty investment. But like Bill had told me, it is a quick turnaround on your investment. You buy produce one day, and in two days, it ought to be sold. The rent was probably going to be my biggest challenge for us here in Sarasota area. Everything was high around here. Where was I going to find anything suitable and, worse yet, affordable? Affordable? That is probably not even a realistic question. Nothing was going to be affordable, in terms of affordable. In other words, everything seems overpriced when you want to rent something in Sarasota. The only way to do this was to do it with a leap of faith. You just have to jump in headfirst, with a whole lot of faith and a whole lot of energy.

Later on here in my story, you will find out one of my other huge leaps of faith I took, not knowing what I was getting into. Even more so than the produce business.

We drove around Sarasota looking for a space to rent, and we even took Sunday afternoon drives just keeping our eyes open for something with a "For Rent" sign in the window or stuck in the grass somewhere. Something that would be suitable to sell produce at. One Sunday afternoon, as we were driving through Osprey, a nice rich little town in the suburbs of Sarasota, suddenly something caught our eye as we were driving by. A little sign in the window said "For Rent," in this little shopping mall with about twelve tenants under the same roof. We debated to keep on driving or turn around and go take a look at it. Well, we were a little ways from home, twenty-two miles to be exact, so we decided it would be better to turn around now than to later regret that we didn't stop. We peeked in through the window and were immediately impressed with the wall-to-wall space. Not a big area, but it felt just about right for us to get started. But rent in a small space here in a shopping mall like this? Would they even allow me to sell produce from this little shopping mall? Rent would no doubt be a killer in this place for sure. But the area seemed good, and the very next day, on Monday, we called the owner of the mall and asked about the price and all. Before he would even talk about the price, he wanted to know what we planned to do with the store. What would we be selling? When I told him we were looking for a place to sell produce from, he fell head over heels in love with what we planned to sell out of this store space. He was as thrilled to see a produce market come in his little shopping center as I was to get started and see what we could do with it. Three thousand dollars a month was an awful lot of money to fork out before we could even start seeing daylight above our cost per month in return money, plus what was yet invested in the produce, jams, jellies, candies, and baked goods. That was not counting the utility cost yet which would be on top of the rent cost. Could we pull this one off? After discussing this over a little bit with Bill Yoder, he encouraged us to go ahead. For the time being, I continued working for Bill during the day. Evenings and into the night, I worked on getting produce-style tables made and set up in the store. It was fun. It was exciting nonetheless.

Once we had the store shelves all in place and ready to fill with fresh produce, my time working for Sutter's ended. I remember very well going after my very first load of produce. Malinda and I. This was a very exciting day, and at the same time, it was also a very strange feeling to go to this wholesale market in Plant City to buy farm-fresh produce, knowing this was going to have to produce much profit in order for this to work out. This was gonna have to feed our family. Put bread on the table. Pay our bills, and also have some fun in the meantime. Rent was going to be high. All this farm-fresh produce was gonna have to produce above all our expenses involved here.

I didn't know yet who the best dealers were or which dealer would sell the best produce or who might have the best prices. We were certainly doing this with a huge leap of faith. But before I could get started, I would need one major tool, and that was I would need something to haul my produce home with. This was just yet another investment before we could see any profit yet. So I took a day off, simply driving around the city of Sarasota, driving by car lots to see what I might find. I did not want a pickup truck because if it rained, my load would get soaking wet. I saw Henry Detweiler do this, and I already knew I didn't want that. I knew what I wanted and so I kept my eye peeled for an Econoline van, something like a work van. I didn't do much driving around when I already spotted this white van the size of a fifteen-passenger van with no passenger seats in it and no windows along the side. It looked almost exactly what I was looking for. I pulled in the parking lot and checked it out. Forty-five minutes later, I walked away from that place owning my own van to haul loads of produce from Plant City, Florida, to our marketplace. This all came together a lot faster and better then even I expected. I was now ready to go after our first load of produce. Being Malinda had worked with fresh produce at Detweiler's Farm Market, I would definitely need to have her go with me to help me with prices and to pick out the best produce for our market. I really had no clue as to how all this produce buying and the markup was all supposed to work yet. This was going to be a real learning experience for me. For us! A real leap of faith, that's for sure. A brand-new field in retail from what I had ever dwelt in before. I knew lawn furniture, but produce was a whole different ball game. It didn't look impossible; in fact, it looked and felt promising to me. The excitement within, probably helped, LOL. It was just going to be something totally different to deal with than I've ever done before.

The day came when Malinda and I went after our very first load of produce with the big old white van. It was exciting. A bit nerve-racking and butterflies in the stomach. Will we be able to survive this market? Can we pull this one off? There was a lot of money invested in the process just to get to our opening day. We borrowed no money. We did it with the cash we had available. We were not these rich folks, but neither were we these poor folks like we were back in Ohio no more either. So at least, we didn't have a loan payment yet on top of the rent and utilities. But it nearly drained our bank account though. If this thing was going to be a total flop, then we were in trouble. If it turned out to well for us, then praise the Lord.

The owner of this shopping mall required some very specific designs for exterior signs on the outside of the building, and they were not the cheap kind either. Another very expensive investment. He required we have boxed letters, as were all attendants of that shopping mall, and they were pretty costly. This was a rich neighborhood, beaches within a mile out behind our store, and lots of famous people living behind us in gated properties. So I guess he thought the stores out front needed to match the neighborhood between us and the beach behind us.

We had our opening day set to open the day after we got our first load of produce. After that first load of produce that we got, we ran every other day, except for Saturdays and Sundays. We were open every day of the week except Sundays. Business took off like a rocket, and we did very well with the store. In fact, it did better than anything I'd done up to this point yet. The community accepted us very well, and we got many comments of how this community needed something like this. For four years, we did produce at this place, and I imagined this might very well be what we would be doing until the day we retired. The job wasn't that hard, and it was a clean atmosphere to work in. I loved it. But wow, was I ever wrong on working here until retirement. I never seen this coming, but God had far greater plans for us. I just didn't know it yet.

It wasn't long until we quickly outgrew the van for hauling produce. I was piling stuff in there from the front of the van to the back of the van, all the way to the ceiling and even on the passenger seat in the front until I couldn't get another box in. It was time for the van to go. It was just not big enough for what we needed anymore. So I sold that van and bought a nice little Isuzu diesel box truck with a reefer cooler mounted on it. This proved to be one of the best investments I could have made for the business. It did us well, and the little truck was fun to drive. I had shelving made on the inside of the box truck along both side walls, and it served as a walk-in cooler when parked right outside on the back side of our building. It cooled while driving it, and when I got to the store, I'd shut down the motor and plug it into electric. My children would sometimes ride along to the produce market with me, even if it meant getting them out of bed at 2:30 in the morning, and I enjoyed that. That meant a lot to me, that they wanted to ride with Dad to the produce market.

The business was doing very well for us. It was a lot of fun but also a lot of work. But life was about to make a sudden and a tremendous change for our family. The produce business was booming, but my walk with the Lord was not so much, and it suddenly caught up with me. I was living a double lifestyle. I wanted to be a Christian, I thought, but at the same time, I wanted to fulfill the lust of the flesh. The Lord is not pleased with a double lifestyle, and it will never work in the long run. It might work for a time, but it will catch up with you eventually, either in this lifetime or in the next, and you better hope it is in this lifetime while there is still time to repent. When I look back on my life now, it nearly blows my mind of how God didn't give up on me years ago already. It is certain in my mind that God was not done with me yet; there is no doubt about that. I am forever grateful for that. God's mercy and His grace covers far more than we humans can fathom. If He can do it for me, he can do it for you. He will do it for anybody, if you accept Him as your Lord.

See, while still living back in Ohio even before we moved to Florida, I had been introduced to an immoral lifestyle: drinking and barhopping almost every weekend with non-Amish friends. It was a habit that was just really hard to kick to the curb. Mostly because we could not tell our friends that we don't do this kind of stuff. So it's very important to choose good friends to hang out with. *Very important!*

See, I had never dealt with the real heart issue of my immoral issues before we moved to Florida. Yes, I had confessed to the Amish church about my double lifestyle, but I knew way down deep inside that I had not truly repented. I didn't know how. So when it got brought to the light, I was basically forced to repent by the brethren of the church and my heart was far from repentance. To be really, *really* honest, I wasn't so much scared of God as I was of the church. I thought surely, everybody else was doing it, and God seemed to be okay with them. Life seemed to go on with them, and it's all good as far as I could tell. So why shouldn't I be okay with it? I made myself to believe that it's not all that bad.

So with time, I wasn't so sure that my double lifestyle was even all that bad. Was God really that upset with me? And still occasionally, I would keep getting this ping in my gut that what I was doing was wrong.

Looking back now, it's very obvious this was the spirit of the Lord pricking my very soul to bring conviction to what I was doing was evil in God's eyes. And I would keep thinking, *I need to quit this. One day, I'll quit.* But it just never happened.

After we had moved to Florida, and we started attending a Mennonite Church and reading the Bible in English version instead of the German version, which was very hard for me to understand to the fullest, it became pretty clear that I needed to repent of my lustful desires of the flesh. But still, I kept pushing it off. *Someday, I will quit*, I reminded myself.

The Bible plainly said it was an abomination to God. One place in the Bible that sticks out to me pretty clearly is in Revelations 21, verses 7 and 8, "He that overcometh shall inherit all things; and I will be his God, and he shall be my son. But the fearful, and unbelieving, and the abominable, and murders, and whoremongers, and sorcerers, and idolaters, and all liars, shall have their part in the lake of fire and brimstone: which is the second death." That's pretty plain language if you ask me. I wanted no part of that fire and brimstone.

Of course, back in Ohio, our Bible reading and preaching was all done in German, which was okay in itself, I suppose, but the message did not come out the same as it did once you learned to read it in the English version for me. Basically, the preaching was preached to be impressed on church rules in mind and what really mattered was whatever the preacher said on Sundays. This is why the fear of the Lord was not as important to me as the fear of man was. In other words, my sinful lifestyle was not as convicting because as long as the ministers didn't find out, I was safe.

The church itself had a lot of man-made rules, and this made it hard to know what was really from God and what was from man. From young up, I was taught we needed to obey the church rules. And I was very aware that if you disobeyed any church standard, that you'd soon have a minister come visit you. I never knew God also came to visit you. His Spirit. This was where real conviction was to come from. But when I started feeling these pings in my stomach, I knew something wasn't right. I was being convicted.

This was back in the day. I know many Amish churches today understand the Spirit of the Lord more today than the church I grew up in back in the day. Although there are still churches around of the very same mindset as what I grew up in, we need to pray for those people. The name Amish simply will not earn you a seat in heaven. It just won't work that way. Although I am forever grateful for my heritage that I grew up with. What was good, I kept with me; what was not good, I left behind me.

Today, I look to the Lord for my strength and for my every need. I search Him in scriptures and I seek Him in prayer.

All right, enough on that for now. So let's go back to our produce business in Florida. Business was booming and I was thoroughly enjoying what I was doing. I could not see myself doing anything else for the time being. I loved what I was doing. We had a very unique little business. And then one day, so suddenly, it was like lighting had struck, and when it struck, it struck so hard that it stopped me right there in my tracks.

God allowed my sinful lifestyle to be known once again, and life would never be the same *ever* again as we had known it. Life would never be the same in my heart and also not in our business *ever*. By God's grace unto this very day, I believe God knew my heart already. To me, it was a total shock, but to God, it was not. God knew the person He wanted me to be years down the road. He knew I was going to turn from my wicked ways at one point in my life, and His mercy and His grace endured until I would truly be able to repent from within my heart. There is just no other way to look at it. God truly is an amazing and all-knowing God. I believe God knew there was a day coming that I would become His son. And that day did come. For me, it did. I'll share that with you little bit later on here.

So here we were, business was booming. I was buying and selling produce by the truckloads. Not semitrucks, but my sixteen-foot Isuzu box truck-loads. I would run an hour north to Tampa, Florida, three times a week, a large indoor wholesale place, and then I'd run about thirty minutes to the east of Tampa, over to Plant City to an all-outdoor whole-sale produce place and fill the truck up to the brim. I made friends with many of those Mexican farmers, wholesalers, and dealers. These people were hard-working produce growers. I really enjoyed what I was doing. I loved my job. I enjoyed the people I got to work with. They were not only dealers, we'd become friends.

But there was one problem. The sin that I had been carrying around with me that I didn't know how to shake on my own was needing to be dealt with.

The ministers of our church were very helpful and concerned with my spiritual well-being, and they wanted what was best for my soul. This was their biggest concern for me. That I would get right with God. They did not want to see me go down a lost soul. Their main concern was "What can we do for a brother who has fallen in sin?" In many ways, it actu-ally felt like everybody was against me. This is what the devil wanted me to believe, that nobody really cared what happened to me at this point.

At this point, I felt God taking my business from me. God can give, and God can take it away in the blink of an eye. See, some people thought I should go get counseling. I didn't think I needed to. Let's get this fixed and taken care of right here in the church. That was my thought. I can't go for counseling out of state with a business as I've got. If anyone really cared, they too would be concerned about my business, right? Just like I was. But they were more concerned about my soul. The rest will all fall in place again Lord willing, in its right timing, they'd told me. Almost immediately, they contacted Fresh Start, a conservative counseling facility in Southern Indiana, and they filled them in about a brother they were dealing with in the church who had fallen in sin.

When the ministers told me they had contacted Fresh Start, I thought I was going to die right there on the spot. Surely I had not heard right. Fresh Start?

This was the last place I wanted to go. Are you kidding me? I knew very little about this place, but still I knew enough that I thought it was for retarded people. Sorry to say that, but that's what I thought this place was for. I didn't think I was retarded, but I knew I did some dumb stuff in my lifetime. I did things I would change if I could.

I'd heard of Fresh Start in the past, and I knew it existed because my cousin had gone through that program several years earlier, but other than that, it was not a place for someone like me to go to. And of course, I did not understand the Fresh Start program as far as that goes. I thought I did, but I didn't.

So here comes my minister, and he pretty much tells me they've contacted Fresh Start, and they have made arrangements to fly out Monday morning to go have an interview with the staff there at Fresh Start. That my wife and I would both be going as a couple, flying with the two of our ministers to have an interview with the staff there. I wanted to run. I wanted to run as fast as I could. I wanted to hide. I wanted this to be just a really, really bad dream. I cannot put in words the feeling I had within myself at this time. This was probably the hardest blow in my face that I had ever experienced in my lifetime ever.

About right now I wanted to be *Mike and Ike: The Runaway Boys.*

Fresh Start?

Come on, I am not that bad of a person. We all make mistakes, right? No one sees their own faults as bad as the next person next to you does. Fresh Start is a place for people with real problems. That's not me. I've been wanting to kick this thing to the curb for a long, long time, and now that I got found out, it'll be easier for me to quit, I was certain of. Let me repent of my failures, the sin that had me bound for so long already, and let me make things right with God and the church so I can go on with life. After all, I got a booming business that cannot survive without my help, and nobody knows that better than I. There was no way Malinda and the children could run this place by themselves while I'm away getting help.

Chapter 9

Eating That Persimmon

Well, so much for my bright ideas. God had different plans. And my desire was to follow God's plan for my life, but sometimes, it takes a lot of courage to give yourself up and actually go do that.

Now, you may wonder why I'm sharing all of these thoughts and struggles of mine with you in a book here. It's because since my conversion, my change of heart, and getting my life right with God, I now realize there are many, many other people out there with the very same struggles that I was in. Deep down inside, they too want out, just like I wanted out. You want to be free from that bondage that's keeping you from feeling totally free, but sometimes, you need others to help you see that and help you out of that rugged old hole you are in. I don't know that I personally can help you, but maybe my story can.

This is my story. This is not a study book of no sort. I felt like if I can share my story, my struggles with you in hopes that you can see you are not alone and that there is hope for you, just like it was for me. I'm hoping my story will be able to give you hope, because for me, the light at the end of the tunnel was, well, to be quite honest, I did not see any light at the end of the tunnel. There was none. But God's ways are not our ways, and His plans are not to harm us, but to give us hope. And so it's very possible you too are not feeling totally free in your life right now. You are not feeling the peace that you desire to have within. You know if you died today, that you were not at peace with God. You just don't have the nerve to talk to anyone about it because what you're doing is too horrible to share with anyone. You know people would look down on you if you told on yourself. You'd be embarrassed of yourself.

A place like Fresh Start, you can freely share with your counselor who will be appointed to you and feel confident sharing with him. It is supposed to stay with him or go no further than to the staff at present. This gives you the support you need to share and pour out your heart to your counselor and go to God with your burdens.

Then again, does it really matter what people think, when you want to fix your problems and get right with Jesus? People ought to rejoice in that, right? Everyone ought to rejoice. Everyone! If there was ever anyone that should get upset with you for getting your life right with Jesus, well, let me assure you, that person is needing help themselves. Instead, all should be rejoicing, rather.

No one ought to go out talking behind your back to their neighbor, "Hey, have you heard?" Those are the people that God would probably *really* like to see go through a program like Fresh Start, right? They are the enemy of God's people. When we read the story of David in Psalms, his enemies were out to kill David because of the sin he had committed, and he cried out to God. The Bible talks about how the angels in heaven rejoice more over the one who was found than the other ninety-nine, because he was lost and now he's found. I used to be ashamed to let people know I went through the program. I am no longer afraid to tell people. I'm rejoicing. And so are the angels in heaven. I don't rejoice in my past; I rejoice of my future in Christ Jesus.

I'm sure there are those out there reading this that can identify exactly what I'm talking about here. It's not easy to share our struggles we face sometimes, but oh, the peace that comes with it is worth it all, afterward. The biggest reason I like to share my story here in this book is because I was once there, right there in that horrible spot of wanting out, but I did not know how. I always thought one day, yes, one day, I would be able to curb this thing on my own and move on in life. What I needed was someone like Fresh Start to walk alongside of me and help me really see how God looks at my sin and what a horrible lifestyle I was actually living. We must see how God looks at sin, not how man looks at it. To me, that sin didn't look as bad, but for some reason, it still made me feel uncomfortable. Why? Because Satan does not bring peace in your heart. It feels dirty. Never clean. God, on the other hand, brings peace and cleanliness. He washes your heart white as snow (Psalm 51:7).

Now that we've graduated from Fresh Start and have moved on with our family life, we now have married children and even got grandchildren. I can see now how God was in this whole thing with us all along. Without Jesus walking alongside of us to help carry the heavy burden that I was carrying and the hurt and shame I had caused upon my family and the church, our friends, our business, there would be no way that I could be where I am today in life. In business. And of course, the ministers of our church who had been right there by my side as well, giving me guidance as they felt best for our situation. I didn't always agree with their plans, but they meant it well. Now looking back, I'm forever grateful for their help and guidance.

Back to the interview at Fresh Start. I could tell you only the good parts of the program, but I'm not going to do that. That would be sugarcoating my real experience here. Although the focus of this story is on me mostly, I, too, wanted to bring in my first initial feelings of facing Fresh Start head-on, what I saw and what I felt and experienced, not only so you can relate with me as I went through this struggle, but also to keep this story interesting, if that makes sense. This is *not* to downplay Fresh Start at all, but mostly, like I mentioned earlier, to keep the story true to my feelings and to keep the story flowing smoothly. I would never discourage anyone from going. In fact, I would encourage you to go if you have been struggling in your life. It's been a huge blessing in my life since.

As we made plans to fly out of Tampa International Airport, flying to Indianapolis International Airport for the interview, we had hired a friend of ours to help our daughters run the produce store while we'd be flying to Indiana. We flew out early in the morning, and we had tickets to fly right back home that very same evening already. This was literally going to be a flying trip. The bishop and one of the ministers flew with Malinda and me. My nerves were so tense and so tight strapped during this trip like I had never before experienced. My hands were plumb sweaty. I could not imagine what an interview at Fresh Start would consist of. What have I gotten myself into? Please, God, let me wake up and find this to only be a very bad dream.

I will probably never forget the picture my wife and I got when we walked through the glass doors at Fresh Start that day. Later on, we shared the very same feelings with each other. There was this Mennonite lady at the front desk who greeted us and handed us a handful of papers to fill out. Reminded me much the same as filling out your health history when you walk into a doctor's office. My picture was taken with a Polaroid camera, and that picture went into the file with those papers that were filled out. This way, when we leave the interview and fly back home and there was mention made of me or my file was pulled out of their drawer later on, they could put a face with this particular file or person. Having said that, all of this was not all that bad. The worst thing for Malinda and me that day were the looks on the faces of the staff men that were walking up and down the hallway, coming and going from every direction it seemed like. These men as they walked past us several times took several glances toward Malinda and me while we sat there in the waiting area. At this time yet, we had no clue that these men were going to be sitting in on the interview with us in that conference room. The only person who looked like he might have any interest in us at all that day was the administrator himself. He had a smile for us every time we made eye contact. The other two staff you would have thought just ate the last persimmon left on the tree. And this is no joke. They never cracked the first smile when they met us. Nor did they smile when we walked into that interview room to meet the staff. When we got called to come to the interview room, I was totally floored to see these two men sitting there around the large conference table along with the administrator, my bishop, and my minister and a few other men. Yes, these two men, the ones who didn't look smart enough to sit in on an interview like this, were *actually* sitting in on this interview, talking with me about my terrible lifestyle I had been living with. I wanted to scream, "Lord, help us all." Make this only a bad, bad dream. For real. It was not what I would have expected from staff who worked in a counseling center. Yet they were there to help people just like me, to get back to real life once again? This place was literally scaring the snoot out of not only me, but also my wife who had done nothing wrong. She was just there for my support and to understand how all this was going to work out. These two men did not look happy to see us or to help me get Jesus back in my life. But you must read on if you want to find out who these two men really were. You will probably be just as shocked as I to learn that one of these men would turn out to be the one chosen to be my *counselor* during my time at Fresh Start. Lord have mercy, right? God works in mysterious ways, huh? I would've never dreamt it. Never!

Go figure.

Now, I know I didn't paint a very pretty picture here of my first experience of entering Fresh Start on my interview. You have to remember, this is my story. Yours might be different. But you must read on to find out the rest of the story.

Have you figured out how God works yet? I haven't either. God works in some very mysterious ways, for sure. I suppose it was exactly what God wanted for me.

The interview lasted longer than it was originally planned because afterward, we were pushed like crazy to get back to Indianapolis airport to catch our flight back home. Ooh, the ride back to the airport was like none other. Our bishop who was with us had a pretty urgent reason to get back home for the next day, I guess. It was pretty important that we don't miss our flight. And he was the one driving the rental car we picked up at the airport earlier on. I've never seen a bishop drive that fast as we did going back to the airport that day. Malinda and I were seated in the back seat of the car, and we could not help but snicker and laugh at his driving. After such a horrible, hard, intense day, we could still laugh. Surprisingly! This was probably the only thing we had to laugh about on this whole trip though. The bishop zoomed our rental car around every car he could get by and even passed cars when it was hardly fit to pass. Even he made comments that it's not even right. Well, we made it safe and we made it on time. We caught our flight, and we were on our way back home to Sarasota.

Back at Fresh Start, before we left that afternoon, I was surprised when Malinda asked me what I thought of this place. My response was, I don't like this place at all. Her reply back to me was that she can't stand this place. After talking some more, we figured out we both felt the same way about the two men on staff that day. We thought they had extremely unfriendly faces that day. Maybe they already knew they were about to interview a fella who was a lost cause. Me. Jesse Kuhns and Davie Wenger were the two sour-faced men that we thought looked more like they were there to *get help* than they were there to help others. Sorry to paint such a picture as this, but this is my story, and I'm writing it exactly as I remember it. But you must continue to read to see more.

*****

After some time back home in Sarasota and some time had passed since the interview, I suddenly felt an urgent nudge from God telling me to go. It felt just like God was standing right beside me, using his elbow, and nudging me in my side.

Go to Fresh Start.

Are you serious?

After such a horrible, unwelcome feeling we had at the interview?

At this very moment, I guess the unwelcome feeling we had earlier on didn't bother me as much as did the idea to get this heavy burden I was currently carrying around on my shoulder behind me.

I was *ready* to get this behind me.

I was ready to get my life right with the Lord. I was no longer questioning God's call for my life. I knew what I needed to do at this point. The feeling. It was very obvious God was telling me to go work on my problems. When God calls, you go, right? Go.

I remember the very moment when I got this real urge within, and I suddenly picked up my flip-open phone as I felt a release of peace in my heart to go. I dialed the number, and I called Bill Yoder, my minister who was walking alongside of me all this time, counseling me one-on-one while I was trying to find my path on which way I was to go while in the midst of this terrible struggle. I called him that morning and said, "Bill, I think I'm ready to go to Fresh Start to help me find my way."

Bill immediately told me to hang tight; he would make a couple phone calls and see what can be done. It wasn't long when he called me back and said Fresh Start said I can come as early as Monday. I was at the store working at the moment. I had just come back with a load of produce.

"But, Bill, what about the produce? What do I do about the business? I can't just up and leave like this."

Business was booming. The bakery needed me. I enjoyed the bread baking during the day. Yes, I baked bread, and I enjoyed it. The business needs me.

Bill told me to not worry about the business, God would provide. And there was a peace that flushed through my whole body. I suddenly felt at peace.

So I pretty much gave it up. I had to. At that very moment, I handed it over to the Lord. "Lord, you have to take care of our business, my wife, and our children."

My flesh was still saying no. My spirit was telling me it will all work out. I could not control my business back in Florida and go for help at the same time. It was either one or the other. One or the other.

When Jesus told the fishermen to follow him, they dropped everything they were doing and followed him. What about their boat? Or their nets? Their fishing gear? And everything else they might have had in the boat that might have been pretty important to them? The Bible doesn't really tell us what became of it. But they immediately followed Jesus (Matthew 4:20).

I had to release my business, and I had to trust that the ministers would help my wife and children make the right choice. This was not easy, believe me. The Lord doesn't tell us that everything will be easy. He just tells us to come, follow Him.

I would be going to Fresh Start myself this time, along with Bill Yoder. My wife and children would stay back and run the store. I actually thought my business would still be there once I finished the program at Fresh Start, but oh, how wrong I was. Never in a thousand years would I have believed what the Lord had in store for us after I was finished with this program. Okay, a thousand years is a long time, but…

I wasn't sure who would run after the produce three times a week because this was a pretty big undertaking. There was just no way Malinda could do that, plus run the store. Oh, how my heart ached within. I was just hoping my time at Fresh Start would be a short-term stay.

I loved my job. I enjoyed everything about it. But I was told not to worry about it, just to go focus on my time at Fresh Start and on my problems, and God would take care of the rest. It was almost more than I could swallow, and yet at the very same time, I did have peace in my heart, knowing I was doing the right thing. I felt a huge burden lifted off my shoulders once I had surrendered my will to go. Little did I know, this would be the last time I would ever see our cute, little produce business in operation. I had put a lot of time and money in that little business, and it was paying off well, but all that didn't mean a hill of beans no more. I had to drop everything I had, just like the disciples did at the boat, I guess. Except for a whole different reason, of course. About the only thing I could take with me was the experience I'd learned in the business. There was a lot of good that I could carry on with me from the business aspect side of it. It was a good experience. Everything else would be gone.

Just so quickly, God took everything from me. Now I say that to say this. I strongly believe if one is living a victorious life for Christ, God will bless you and your business because living for Christ will put you into a position where you will do whatever it is to honor and bless God, your Lord. And God will bless you for that. But on the other hand, if you are living in sin, be assured your sin will find you out. That's what the Bible tells us (Numbers 32:23). And I suppose it is better that your sin is found out now, while there is still time to make it right. Otherwise, when Jesus returns and you have never repented and you face Him face-to-face and He has to tell you, "I never knew you, depart from me" (Matthew 7:23).

So in saying all that, I believe God can give and God can take away. And he can take it away quickly. It doesn't mean just because a tornado came through your area and destroyed everything you had, that you must have some hidden sin in your life. Or a fire took everything you had, you had sin in your life that had not been dealt with yet. This could be true, but only you know that for sure. Because go read the book of Job in the Bible. That is one powerful true story of a man that Satan had plans to destroy. But God told Satan he could not take Job's life, but he could take everything else, and Job would still trust whole heartily in Him, the Creator. It will just about blow your mind when you read the first couple of chapters of Job of the many hundreds of animals and servants he owned and just so quickly, everything was taking from him, including his family. That was a tremendous loss for Job. But Job did not leave God, and Job was later restored back more than he had in the beginning.

Now, this chapter was a difficult chapter for me to write in more ways than one. For one, to write it in a way so that you, the reader, can totally understand what I'm trying to explain felt difficult. I hope this makes sense to you. The other, it was a total embarrassment to write this chapter, but I know for a fact there are many out there that can understand exactly what I went through. So take courage, take that step in faith, and go walk with God.

Chapter 10

Fresh Start

Bill Yoder booked a flight for him and me. He flew with me to Indiana to the Fresh Start facility and helped me settle in somewhat, and then I didn't see anything of him anymore. He was gone. I didn't even get to say goodbye. I believe he flew back home the next day, but I'm not exactly sure. Well, the rest, like they say, is history. Our lives would never be the same ever again. God had a different plan for us. It was a really tough time for all of us. My throat was dry. My stomach was in a knot. My hands were sweaty. I just wanted to go to bed and get up the next morning, hoping this was all just a really bad dream. But when I got back up the next morning, the sun came back up just like usual. The breeze blew lightly, just like it did yesterday. The smell of that fresh Florida smell, like only Florida can, still had that good Florida scent in the air. But I wasn't there anymore to smell it. I was in Indiana now. My dream had not vanished though; life was still real. I had to face life head-on.

Of course, when I left our Florida home and our business behind to go get help, to get my life back on track with God, I thought at that time that I would be returning back home pretty soon again, to continue our produce and bakery business again. What I didn't know was that that would never happen. Of course, I was not aware of that at this time yet. I'm not sure that anyone really knew that. One thing that helped me a lot and allowed me to get some peace in my heart to move ahead and go to Fresh Start was something that Bill Yoder told me before I left Florida. Bill, my former boss at Sutter's where I worked for several years, knew I was struggling to leave our prosperous little produce business behind in the hands of my wife and children, and likely, they too would be coming to join me at Fresh Start a little later on. There was a lot of hurts there that we, as a family, needed to work through because of my failures in life. The double lifestyle I had been living. So the one thing that Bill told me before I left was "Nealie, you have a lot of experience in business. You grew up doing business, and once things get back to a more normal routine again after your time at Fresh Start, you can always start your business back up again, if you trust in Jesus. Jesus gives hope. Jesus *is* hope. You're smart enough to do that."

He told me that he had confidence in me I could do that. This gave me courage. This gave me hope. I needed to hear something positive in the midst of this horrible trial I was going through at the moment. Leaving my business behind. My family. It was nearly more than I could bear. The feeling.

There are always people out there who want to tear you down. They wish for the worst of you. There were those who confessed to be Christians, but they display real hate toward me because I had failed in life. For some people, if you fail in life, in their minds, you're always a failure. Once a failure, always a failure. They wish the worst for you. But Jesus is our healer. Jesus gives hope. His hands are reaching out toward you. Come.

I was dreading to face this road head-on, but I knew there was light up ahead, because a few people told me so. I was also looking forward to get my life back on track with God in a way that I probably never really ever had yet.

One night, while in a deep sleep in the middle of the night before I left to go to Fresh Start, I had an experience I hope I will never forget. Suddenly, in the middle of the night, I woke up feeling like Jesus was right there in the room with me. Something felt very present and near to me. I still don't know exactly what happened, whether I was in a dream and woke up or if it was a vision I was in and I woke up. I was in a solid sleep when I suddenly slipped out of bed and got on my knees and gave my life to the Lord right there in the middle of the night. I remember doing it, and after I prayed this prayer, I slipped back in bed and I don't remember lying awake long after that. I soon fell right back to sleep. But it was very real, and it meant something to me.

I prayed the prayer of Psalm 51:

> Have mercy upon me, O God, according to thy lovingkindness: according unto the multitude of thy tender mercies blot out my transgressions. Wash me throughly from mine iniquity, and cleanse me from my sin. For I acknowledge my transgressions: and my sin is forever before me. Against thee, thee only, have I sinned, and done this evil in thy sight: that thou mightest be justified when thou speakest, and be clean when thou judgest. Behold I was shapen in iniquity; and in sin did my mother conceive me. Behold, thou desirest truth in the inward parts; and in the hidden part thou shalt make me to know wisdom. Purge me with hyssop, and I shall be clean: wash me, and I shall be whiter than snow.

Daily, I had been seeking the Lord in prayer and searching for restitution. I wanted my life cleaned, and I wanted to have a normal family life again. I thought the world of my family, but it felt like I was about to lose them if I didn't truly seek God with all of my wisdom. With all of my might. And all of my strength. I needed change. And I wanted change. That is how I think I found God and fell on my knees that night. Maybe it was the prayer I had. Maybe it was the talk I had with Jesus that evening before I fell asleep for the night, and Jesus showed up when my heart was ready to receive him. I don't know exactly why it happened as it did. That very next day, I told Bill Yoder of the experience I had, and he told me to write it on a piece of paper or in a journal of how it all went so that I would never forget. He told me Satan does not like experiences like this, and he would very likely attack me here in the near future with thoughts and doubts that this experience I had was not for real. To put doubts in my mind so that I won't believe. So I did. I wrote everything down in my journal to remember. Till today, I remember it as if it was just the other night. I can actually not really describe just how it felt. I've never went through something like that before or since. But I know Jesus was real.

So here I was, at the bottom end of the year of 2006, I entered the program, the counseling center there at Fresh Start, in hopes I would be in and out of the program in about eight months to a year, like most others that went through there. Well, that didn't go as I hoped either.

After I was there one month into the program and also right on my birthday, something horrible happened there at Fresh Start. Abe Knepp, the founder of Fresh Start, was flying his airplane out of the small local airport just a couple miles behind Fresh Start when he suddenly crashed in a field and was killed. I had only known Abe for one month. Only got to hear him preach one sermon at Fresh Start Chapel. His friend and often copilot Dave Swartz was also flying one of Abe's other little planes. They would be flying next to each other to Kentucky or Tennessee somewhere where Abe was to leave one plane to get inspected or worked on and then he would fly back with Dave in the other plane. I believe Dave said he actually saw Abe do a sharp U-turn with his plane as he went down behind some trees. Abe's plane was all rolled up into a ball and scattered over this open muddy field down below. I still wonder if Abe tried an emergency crash landing, but when the wheels hit that soft dirt in this field, the wheels, instead of rolling like they normally would, grabbed and stuck to the mud, and the plane did the nose flip and just rolled into a ball.

Us guys, referred to as residents at Fresh Start, were out working in the shop when one of the staff members, Jesse Kuhns, gathered all of us residents into a circle for prayer and then informed us of the plane crash, that Abe was in the plane and was killed. We immediately all got in a van and drove over to the crash site. We weren't allowed into the open field up close, so we just watched from the road. That was the first and only time I ever witnessed the site of a plane crash like this. Being this happened on my birthday, it's easy for me to remember what day this happened.

Abe Knepp was not only the founder of Fresh Start, but he was also the bishop at Fresh Start Chapel.

This was a tough time for Fresh Start because Abe was the backbone for this counseling center, and how was it to survive without him? But God saw it through. No mountain was ever too big for God.

Well, so much for thinking I might be able to graduate Fresh Start in eight months. You can say that three times over. Yup. I ended up serving twenty-three months at that place. One month shy of two full years. This was crazy. Far beyond what I ever expected.

Now after I graduated and time had moved on, I tell people, I do not believe I really needed to stay that long in the program. I knew where my heart was at, but of course, the staff did not. My family did not. But here is what I tell people now, by staying that long in the program, I learned some very valuable lessons that I would not have learned, had I not stayed in the program this long. For that, I'm forever grateful. Since we have graduated Fresh Start, I have told some folks that I would not trade a million dollars for what I've learned while being in this program, it was life changing for me. But I would not give a penny to go through it again, LOL. It was really tough, but really good for me. The program.

It was very intense in a lot of ways, but I look at it this way. God put me in this program to test me for a reason. Would I be able to pass the test? Could I endure my time there for nearly two full years with no pay to help support my family? If I could not pass this test, I would probably not pass the next test God was preparing for me in the future. I don't know my future, so I must remain strong in the Lord. I must pass the test that God puts in front of me. It is a daily thing for all of us. Look at the beautiful, touching story of Joseph in the Bible, who had to endure prison time for something he didn't even do, to pass that test in order for God to see if he would be the leader in a country where God needed him in. God was preparing Joseph to be the one in charge of a great drought coming.

Sometimes, God will put us through the fire, a trial, to see if we can pass the test, in preparation for whatever it is that he is preparing you for the next step in your life. Will you be able to pass the test? While writing this, we are currently still members here at Fresh Start Chapel nearly sixteen years later, because we feel this is where God wants us, not a part of Fresh Start Training Center, but members of the church. The residents and staff from the training center come over every week and join us for Sunday church services and Wednesday evening prayer meeting. So here I get to see and meet with all the residents that come and go through the program, and I will tell especially those that sometimes are struggling to stay focused or committed in the program, that look, God probably has you in here for a reason. Will you pass that test? If you can't pass this test, you probably won't pass the next test either. I can assure you, it can get tough, hard, and difficult, but if you put your trust in the Lord, I can promise you, you will come out a better stronger person than the day you entered Fresh Start. Is this what you want? This is what makes it worth it all. This is what makes it exciting. That was my goal from the day I entered Fresh Start, and I can honestly say, I feel like I finished well.

During the time I was there in the program, it was an indefinite stay. You stayed until your counselor thought you were ready to leave or fully commit to serving God. There were no ifs, ands, or buts. It also had a play in with the wife or family too when they were ready to get back to doing life together without being under the safeguard of Fresh Start staff walking right beside you day in and day out. Was the family ready to trust you to be true to them? Was I the person God intended me to be?

Back to the day I entered myself into the program, I had made up my mind to fully surrender myself to the program, honor the staff, and do the best that I knew how. I was committed to get my life back to God. I was done with this double standard of living. It did nothing for me, but cause pains and heartaches, not only for myself, but even more so to the rest of my family.

The staff, of course, saw all flavors of residents come and go through this place, and I understood that part. They saw almost every kind of person you can imagine come through there, some desiring help, others only there either because their family asked them to go or the church encouraged them to go. They saw single men come through there. They saw couples come through there that really do not want to be there. And then they also saw men come through there that were actually looking to get their life back on track with God. They saw men come through the program who kind of learn how to play the system to just get through there and get out of there, because they really didn't want to be there in the first place. Some residents learned how to play the system so well that they seemed all into it, doing the talk and walking the walk. These types of young men make it very difficult for the ones that are actually trying to be honest and desiring help. They were practically forced by their ministers from back home to go or their accountability person persuaded them to go. Or the family persuaded them to go. They didn't really choose to go on their own. I know the feeling. I know the pressure. I, too, was somewhat persuaded to go, but my ministry never did push me. My family never pressured me to go. They gave me time. Lots of time. They left it totally up to me, and I'm sure they were praying for me every day. No one pushed me to go but God, and when he did, I knew I needed to go. Suddenly, one day, I found that peace deep down in my heart to go. My spirit was ready, but my flesh was weak, and I still wanted to wake up one morning and realize this was only a terrible dream and this was not true. Me? Go to Fresh Start?

But now that I was here, I was going to put my all into it. I had no intentions to do this only halfway. I was going to do it right. I had made up my mind that I was going to cooperate with the staff and do my best. If they said jump, I was going to jump. If they said swim, I was going to swim. I knew it was going to be a struggle because I was now under their authority. I was no longer running my produce business. I could feel the battle coming on. I was here. This was where I was going to grow in the Lord.

I had a beautiful family that I could not afford to lose. I could hear God's still, small voice and I was trying to make sense of it. Could the staff at Fresh Start help me, guide me, to the path that leads to this victory in Jesus?

Here I was, putting my all into this program. I put my everything into my daily studies and classes that we residents had before us. And we had many. We had our Bible reading every morning from 6:00 to 7:00 before breakfast, reading four assigned chapters every day. Our daily routine was every morning out of bed, do your hygiene and straight to the training room for Bible reading. Every morning. Sometimes, it was a real battle to keep my eyes open. In the twenty-three months that I was there, I was never once called out for falling asleep during Bible reading. If you got called out, you might got asked to stand. Stand alone, while the others could remain sitting. It was meant for a punishment, and even more so, so you could stay awake. Or worse yet, you got to sit on a pointed chair, something like a milking stool, if you know what that was. Some residents did well if they didn't get called out at least once every morning. I was determined to train myself in to do my job and do it right. Every resident read the same chapters while we sat at our assigned seats in the training room. Then at 7:00 on the minute, we all went to the kitchen for breakfast. At 8:00, we then all went back into the training room along with a staff member leading us in an open discussion about the Bible reading we just had. In my twenty-three months at Fresh Start, I will have to say, this was the greatest highlight of my time there. Reading four chapters every morning. I learned so much stuff that I had absolutely no knowledge about, that is right there in the Bible, and then having this open discussion every morning after breakfast was just another highlight because it allowed for open discussion if anyone had questions about anything we read or didn't understand. It brought out many good things that I had no understanding of.

Because I was putting my *all* into this program and I was doing my best to respect the authority who were over me there, this was going right in the line of those that also knew how to play the system just so they could get through this program and back out again but had no real change of heart in mind. So Jesse Kuhns, my counselor, thought I was one of those players and that I was not going to fool him. That's what he thought. The better I did, the harder he got on me. For example, every Wednesday was what we called Social Gram Day. As residents, we had a paper where all the residents' names were on. Beside each name, from Wednesday to the following Wednesday, we had to put something beside each resident's name of something we seen he was struggling with during that week. Something he did that he should not have, even if it was just something plain stupid. Then each resident, along with all of the staff members, sat in the training room, and usually two residents were put on the hot seat. We residents then took turns sharing what we had written down beside each name. Here is an example of how we would share: "Nealie, I love you, but I noticed you procrastinated in getting your work done on Monday of this week." Or maybe they noticed someone got angry about a certain issue. Once everyone had shared what they wrote down, then one person was chosen to get picked on. This means they got drilled with questions or hammered as to why he did so and so. Or what made you do that.

It was *the* single hardest, and I cannot stress this point enough, the *hardest* part of the program at Fresh Start. I absolutely dreaded this day. Actually, to be really honest, I hated this day. I dreaded Wednesdays even if I was not the one on the hot seat that day. I hated that day. For me, it was a dark day in the program. And the darkest days yet were when I was put on the hot seat. First off, I tried to respect all authorities and residents the best I knew how. I tried to keep in mind to do my work out in the shop in the afternoons as unto the Lord and not unto men. I was not getting paid to work here, all these twenty-three months I was there. It was a battle for me at times, and I had to work really hard at it to be totally okay with making this the Lord's work. But on Social Gram Days, it was a tough day for me, because half of the time, the residents could not find one single fault to write down beside my name from one week to the next, which meant they would need to skip lunch. Yup, if you missed even just one name, you skipped lunch. It was mandatory to write something on everyone. No one wanted to skip lunch. Not only did you have to skip lunch, but during this time, you were required to be in the study room studying or reading your Bible while the others were out there enjoying a good cooked lunch. Many residents had to miss lunch because they could not find anything to write beside my name. Well, when I got on the hot seat, this was a really tough day for me. I got drilled even harder by the staff for the reason no one could find any fault in me. I got accused of playing the system so well that the residents could not find any fault in me. That's what the staff would tell me right there in front of all the residents. It made me feel and look like a fool. I already felt bad that they had to skip a meal, and now I'm getting drilled to the core for doing my best. Not only that, back in my counselor's room, I'd get hammered once again. And that hurt. I was up against a rock and a hard place. There was nothing I could do about it but to swallow it and be gracious toward the staff. I knew why I was getting drilled like this was because of the experience they had with real players in the system before. And worst part for me was I had no answer for them. I would simply go blank for answers. I was doing my daily job the best I could do. I was trying to respect the staff. I had made up my mind before I ever came to Fresh Start that I wanted to seek and walk with God the whole time I was there, and I meant it. I did not want to go back living my old lifestyle. I had given my heart to the Lord before I ever came to Fresh Start, and I was not planning to fall back in my old ways. What was I to do? I was kept at Fresh Start a whole lot longer because my counselor thought I was one of those players who knew how to play the system and I was not about to fool him. I knew deep down in my heart that I was not there to play the system. I was there for change. Yes, of course I knew I was made of flesh. I knew I could fall again. I also knew if my heart was right with God, whenever I would fall again, I would get right back up again and move on. When a righteous man falls, he gets back up again (Proverbs 24:16). He doesn't stay down. And then again, God possibly had a larger plan for me. For that, I can be forever grateful. My longer term than normal at Fresh Start was not a waste of time. It was not easy. It was hard, but through it all, God was good.

After some time, I'm not sure just when it was anymore, it was time for Jesse and his family to go on sabbatical for several month. This really lifted my spirits for a moment. I saw hope. I felt a small urge of hope. Will this have an effect on my stay here, now that my councilor was leaving? Could this be when I would be released from the program? As tough as Jesse was with us, Malinda and I, we still enjoyed Jesse and his wife for our counselors for the most part. Jesse was a man who was hard to figure out; I'm not going to lie, he was. At the same time, as

Malinda and I talked between ourselves, we were not so sure we wanted to be changing counselors once they left on sabbatical, and we would possibly still *not* be released from the program. This was a tough time for us, and now to get a new set of counselors was going to be even tougher on us as a family. Was there any light at the end of this tunnel? Would this ever end? I was hoping, *maybe I forgot to pray*, but I know I was hoping this could surely be a time that the staff could see fit to let us graduate from the program. Surely? Was this going to be the breaking point for us here? I absolutely did not have the nerve to ask my counselor about it. I could never tell if he truly liked me or sort of had it in for me. Deep down inside, if I told the truth, I think he either did not like me very much or he simply had it in for me, if that makes sense. So, asking him such a question as to whether we might be able to graduate would only have him question me harder and make me feel like a fool for asking. So I talked it over with my wife. We both did not know how this was going to be handled yet. So when we found out that Laben and Susie Yoder would consider taking us on until Jesse would be back again, we were really excited. Okay, that does not really cut it. We were overjoyed to learn they might take us on. At the same time, it was a real letdown for me. What happened to that hope I had felt earlier on? Learning we would not be graduating at this point was not a good feeling, but I was very thrilled to know Laben might step in to help us to move on ahead. So there was still a tinge of hope there. Laben had been the only one who could always lift my spirits if anybody could. It was not very long into our counseling sessions with Laben and Susie when I could already see and feel light at the end of the tunnel. My spirit was being lifted every day to a higher ground. God was good. Things progressed from there on out, even though we had still not graduated by the time Jesse's family came back from their sabbatical. Both Malinda and I knew we did *not* want to go back to Jesse and his wife for counselors. We pleaded to keep Laben to finish us out. Laben's job title at Fresh Start was not a counselor, but he had other responsibilities rather. But during our time of going through the program, Laben and his wife Susie and my wife and I became best friends. So they considered taking us on and decided they would do just that. We were thrilled. Things kept looking up from there on out, although it took some time again, but it was not hard to feel Laben's heartbeat for us. I believe Laben was able to see something in us that Jesse could not. So now, backing up a bit again before Jesse left to go on sabbatical.

When we entered the program, I thought I was going to be out of there in eight months to a year. Surely. But my counselor was a tough one. Really tough. Tough but good. My wife and I learned to appreciate them. They worked with us almost daily. But when the eight-month time came around and I had not felt or heard the first thing about being released, I was disappointed and discouraged. Who wouldn't be? Seriously? Do I say something or do I just remain calm and patient within? Is it better to remain quiet or to say something? So one day, for my counseling session, Jesse and I drove over to the City Park and sat on one of those swing sets with a roof over it, sitting under the shade of trees in the park. That's where we had our one-on-one chat that day. I don't remember our conversation in particular of that day except it got to where it worked out perfectly for me to bring in that one question that was weighing heavy on my mind to ask. That question that had my heart beating at a higher rate of speed than normal. I didn't like the feeling I was feeling. It was that eerie feeling of being scared to ask my personal counselor a question. Shouldn't have been that way, but it was. Jesse was the type of person that could make you feel like a fool for asking him a question. The type of person that would have you regretting that you even asked the question. And that's exactly what happened right there at the park. Instead of answering my question, he would put that question right back into your lap. So he asked me, "What do you think? Do you feel like you're ready?"

"Well, yes, I feel ready."

And again, he asked me, "Why do you think you're ready?"

And it ended up exactly where I wished I'd never asked the question. All I wanted was to know, what does he think? Should've been a safe place to ask, right? Your councilor. A simple yes-or-no answer. And why did he think I was not ready? What did I still need to work on? I've been here for ten months now, and he still did not think I was ready to graduate. And he would leave me hanging without an answer. I knew no more after I'd asked, and I was now only feeling even worse than before. I had to deal with it until the next session, which would not be until the next day. But there was never an answer for me, and it was a real letdown for me. And then there were some really good days too. Other days were really hard. This particular day was really hard. I was not seeing any light at the end of the tunnel during this time in my life. Not even after being there for ten whole months now. And then it happened again. God sent a messenger to me again in the midst of a dark day in my life. That very afternoon as I was out there in the shop, working on lawn furniture, while running the chop saw that afternoon, Laben Yoder came walking out, and he walked right over to where I was working to see how I was doing. Now remember, this was before the time of sabbatical for Jesse where they took some time off, away from Fresh Start. I always cherished the times Laben came by to chat with me. Laben always had a way to lift my spirits. He had a way to bring hope in the midst of the dark trial I was going through. That day, he lifted my spirits again. It was just amazing how God always worked this out in just the perfect timing. In just the right time, Laben would come out to the shop in the afternoon and just chat with me for a bit. Didn't happen all that often, but I certainly cherished every bit of it. Rather than tear me down, he had a way to lift my spirits. Jesse was a good friend to me in other ways, but he could also tear you up in our counseling session and walk away leaving you hanging until the next day. It didn't bother him a bit. I was a hurting man. My family was hurting. We needed help. We needed someone to walk alongside of us and help us find our path. Find God. We didn't need to be left hanging on the line fending for ourselves. I'm not going to sugarcoat this story and tell you only the good parts of going through this program. I'm here to give you the perfect picture of a real trial, a real test of a family that went through a hard time as we searched our hearts to find freedom and a brand-new heart in Christ. Remember earlier on, I mentioned that sometimes God puts us through the test? Maybe he is testing you to see if you can pass this test. Are you going to pass the test? If you can, then God can possibly use you for the next step he is preparing you for. Who knows what that may be. A future preacher? Or just that perfect Godly father and perfect husband? Maybe a future counselor for Fresh Start? Yup, that has happened time and time again. Numerous other things. Remember, God has a plan for your future. He is preparing you for that next step in your life. Another perfect, true story I want to tell you about that absolutely blew my mind that actually happened one afternoon as I stepped out of my counseling session with Malinda. Not only did this just happen, but it was also an answer to a prayer. A prayer that God answered within just a few minutes after I had prayed it. And it strengthened my faith tremendously. That story will be in this next chapter.

Chapter 11

The Note

I learned a new thing about prayer that I guess I never really thought about. For as long as I remember, growing up, I thought you need to fold your hands, close your eyes during prayer, and do it silently. That's just how my parents always did it, except for when Dad would read out loud from a little prayer book every morning before breakfast and every evening before bedtime. That's how the church always did it. Close your eyes, fold your hands, and pray. And of course in German. God can only understand the German prayers, I thought. Because you had to be Amish in order to make it to heaven. That's what we were taught. That was how I thought God could hear and understand you. How terribly wrong I was.

But I appreciate a new thing that Jesse taught me, and I've used it ever since and maybe even in different ways. We were not to take the first step off the property of Fresh Start or it was an automatic send-me-home ticket. You step off the property, you get sent home. That was unless you had permission from your counselor to do so. The blacktop road that came up along the side of Fresh Start property turned into a dead end just a skip and a hop to the north. Going south, it was another skip and a hop to a stop sign at the end of the road. Jesse was one who was all for exercising, and for some odd reason, he thought I should get up early before breakfast every morning and run up and down this little side road several times just like he was doing every morning. Now, I was *not* a runner. Could hardly even play volleyball no more because of my bad knees. I've been having knee problems for a while already, and at times, they would hurt day and night. Then the pain would go away for a spell again. Sometimes, I wouldn't feel it for some time. But I couldn't be working bent down on my knees for half a day since my knees would start hurting so bad that I could hardly stand back up straight without moving like an old, old man. Inside, I did not feel like an old man, but working on my knees made me feel like an old man really fast. And the pain would last for a week or more after that. I'm then reminded of why some people say it is no fun to get old. Aches and pains. But I'm not even old yet. You need to be old before your knees should start aching, not? For me, a real bad one was doing gazebo floors, which I did a fair amount of. I spent a lot of time on my knees doing the gazebo floors, and that hurt my knees pretty bad, but I dared not say anything to the Fresh Start staff, except maybe

Jesse, my counselor, and I tried to grin and bear the pain. I actually enjoyed doing the floors, if it was not for my knees. It got bad enough that I actually worried I would be needing knee surgery before it was all over yet. But then other times, it seemed when there was rain coming, this too would bring on pain in my kneecaps. To this day, I still have not had knee surgery yet. I still have the same problem though and, at times, enough to make me groan. I get the feeling sometimes that it might not be my kneecaps going out but simply the dreadful disease of arthritis. I'm afraid that is what it might actually be. But I don't really know what arthritis is supposed to feel like either. But nevertheless, I told Jesse I was not able to run because of my knees. I immediately saw the look on his face and that smirk, that he highly doubted my honesty. He encouraged me to go anyway. And if you know Jesse, these four words barely came out, but just groaningly slow, "Just go do it. You can do it." And he would not say it in a loud forceful way either. He always did it with many grunts, groans, twists, and turns and in a low soft-voice type of way, like only Jesse could do. It was the sound of "I don't think you're being very honest with me," or he thought I was just making this stuff up.

Like I said before, only he could do it like that. Ooh, but I did not want my knees to hurt again. I told him I couldn't do it. Just couldn't. He doubted me again, and he was not afraid to let me know he was doubting me. I don't think he ever did believe me. So then he asked that I go walk up and down the road. While walking, he wanted me to use all my time in prayer or memorizing scripture verses while I was walking. To use my time wisely. Not to do it just to be out there walking. I wasn't sure what I was getting myself into again. I was nervous. I was scared. I was all for going out there and walk, but I wasn't sure about the prayer time. I enjoyed going on walks. Still do. But I wasn't sure how I was to concentrate on prayer while I'm walking up and down the road with all kinds of distractions on either side of me. Fresh Start on one side of the road. Olan, a furniture drawer factory, on the other. But I was willing to give it a try. I told him I would give it a try, and so I was going to do it. After I started walking every morning, soon, a few others started doing the same thing. I found it to be a really good time to get outside and refresh myself of the pressure I was under already. Breathe in, breathe out. And air out. In the winter, the days were shorter, and it stayed dark for a lot longer in the mornings. During the summer months, it was already daylight when I got up. So by saying this, I'm saying I could get up before our six o'clock Bible reading time and walk up and down the road while it was still dark outside. I liked that because others couldn't see me so well.

But I learned to really appreciate this time with God alone. Just me and God. I learned to walk and pray. I learned that I could walk and be in prayer, and I never noticed the distractions on either side of me. I could get so deep in prayer while I was walking up and down that little stretch of blacktop that I wasn't ready to quit when it was time to quit. I learned to understand the fact that God loves when we pray to Him. I could feel a connection. A connection I had never really felt before. Now years after graduation, I still love to pray out loud to God wherever I might be, in my little woodworking shop all by myself. On the bus when traveling, I pray. Wherever I'm at, if I think of a need of something, I'll pray.

Now to go back to the reason of this chapter, that little note. Now that I enjoyed my prayer time with God alone, there was this one particular day when Jesse had Malinda and I do our own session time together, in our own little room all by ourselves, discussing whatever we felt the need to talk about, without his presence. Learning to work things out on our own without the help of a counselor. Remember, this was still before Laben and Susie took over counseling us. As much as I looked forward to these special days alone with my wife, it could also get pretty tense at times, learning to hear each other out, because we didn't always see eye to eye.

Later on, when Laben was helping us work through some of these tough situations, he told me something that has stuck with me unto this day. I suppose I will never forget it as long as I live. He said one thing I have to remember is, God made man and He made woman. He wired men's brain different than women. So I have to remember that the reason my wife sometimes thinks differently than I do, no matter how much sense it makes to me, God made her to see things in a different way, sometimes, than man sees. I have to just accept that. Her way of thinking might work out just the same as my way of thinking does at the end. Just be okay with it.

I never forgot that.

So on this particular day, as Malinda and I were sitting in our little room discussing something, there was something we didn't agree on, but to this day, I cannot tell you what our conversation was anymore. Probably a good thing I don't, LOL. But I remember we had a pretty tense session for both of us. Just the two of us. When our time was up, where she needed to leave and I needed to get to the shop, we were absolutely not finished with our conversation. I absolutely hated to part ways like this and leave it hanging like this and walk away. But we had no choice but to quit and call it a day. If I walked out in the shop a minute late, I was going to get a chewing out by the shop foreman, because he knew exactly what time I was to be in the shop. This just tore at the core of my heart to leave our session unfinished like this until the next day when we could meet again. I did not have a good feeling about our conversation. An unfinished conversation. This just absolutely tore me up. I had to quickly say my goodbyes and get out in the shop. I would not see Malinda until the next day at about the same time. But our session wouldn't be one-on-one like it was today. It would be with Jesse and his wife, which meant Malinda and I could not finish whatever it was we were talking about. My heart was simply feeling torn apart at the moment. I walked out to the shop, and there was only one way to get peace in my heart and that was to pray. Pray like I had learned to pray when I was walking by myself out on my early morning walks, talking to God alone. The saws, the routers, the air nailers a-popping, and all this racket going on, no one could hear me if I actually prayed out loud audibly. I could not go through the remainder of this day feeling this bad on the inside. My heart was torn. So I walked over to my station where I was working on porch swings. I had my back turned toward everybody else. So what do I do but pray? I had my back to everybody else, the saws running, and so I just prayed out loud audibly. I prayed to God and told Him I would just like to see Malinda just one more time before she went home, quickly. I knew it was impossible, but I needed to get rid of this sickening feeling I was feeling inside. I wanted peace within. I was not allowed to step outside of the shop without a reason and holler at Malinda just to speak a few words. These were the shop rules. I was to stay in my work area. I prayed that God would grant me to somehow be able to see Malinda's face just one more time before she leaves. She never comes out to the shop after our sessions, but if the large garage door was open, I could often peek out there and wave her goodbye. But this day, the garage door was closed. I would not be able to see her drive off. I just cried out to the Lord for help. He knew what I was feeling. So I prayed. I pleaded with the Lord to let me just at least see her face before she goes home, if that was possible. I guess I thought seeing her face would speak volumes to me. Her facial expression could give me the peace I needed.

I had not more than finished praying when Malinda walks in through the shop door and gives me a little note. I cannot tell you what I felt right at that moment. But as she walked away, my burdens were lifted just like that. It was as though Jesus had just reached down through the thick clouds and taken the heavy weight I was carrying, right off my shoulders right there. Her facial expression was just what I needed to see. Her face didn't looked burdened. Just that quickly, God had answered my prayer. Never before at *any time* would Malinda have the nerve to walk in the shop to even as much as tell me something, much less hand me a note. You have to remember, we were on a pretty tight string here at Fresh Start while we were in this program. Good for the heart and good for the soul, but hard on the flesh. But God answered my prayer right in the midst of this. You talk about strengthening my faith in God. That right there did.

Had I not prayed, would she have walked in anyway? You know, those kind of questions will go through your mind afterward. But I will choose to believe God answered my prayer right then and there, right when I needed it the most. Just that little bit of seeing her made all the difference for me to make it through until the next day. God loves when we have a personal relationship with Him. Sometimes, I wonder if we maybe don't talk to God enough. Jesus probably talked to God like this and even much more than we do today. Just like we talk to our earthly father. Talk to God. God will listen.

And I don't, for the life of me, even remember what that note she handed me was about anymore. But my faith had been strengthened for sure. God is real.

Chapter 12

Graduated Fresh Start

When I graduated Fresh Start, we had no money in the bank. No extra cash. The money in our wallet was all we had. Didn't own a house or any land. Didn't even have a place to rent yet. And we had seven hungry children to feed. Had one vehicle for ourselves and a car for our oldest daughter so she could go to the youth functions and to work and the clothes on our back. That was it. Our business we had in Florida was no more. It had been sold soon after I had left to go to Fresh Start, totally out of my control. It could have felt like a sad, *sad* day for us to start out with hardly anything to our name. Except we were starting out with a brand-new fresh start. A brand-new fresh start in life. We had lost all our earthly possessions, but we had everything we needed to start out fresh. Fresh out from scratch. We were now refreshed with the armor of God in our hearts, and we knew we were in good hands. If the Lord choose to do so, He could multiply everything we touched with His blessings and for His glory. That was truly my goal in life from here on out. I was confident God would supply for our every need because He already knew everything He had planned for our future ahead.

Fresh Start allowed me to start a new job just before I actually graduated so that I would be able to support our family. So this meant during the day, I would go to work at Graber Steel and Fab for work and then return to the training center for the night. In the evenings, when it worked out to do so, Laben and Susie would still counsel with us. I started working at Graber Steel and Fab located near Odon, Indiana, owned and operated by an Amish family. When I started working there, there were around twenty-five or so employees working there, all Amish except a few of us drivers to bring in the employees every morning and take them back home in the evenings again. During the day, we drivers also worked in the welding shop, a steel manufacturing facility.

After two years of being totally depended on Fresh Start to support us, we had a whole new world to learn over again. Like I mentioned earlier on, before I came to Fresh Start, we had a booming business that was making us more money than we had ever seen before. But because of sin in my life, God wiped everything off the slate for us. The business was sold while I was in the program, and I had no say so in the matter at all. I had to surrender that completely to God. We owned two properties in Florida with a house and outbuildings on each property. Financially, we were doing pretty good, we thought, but about the time that I decided to go get help was when we had just bought our second property, which was just under $500,000. A half-million dollar home in Florida to its best. It was our dream home with a seven-car garage, not attached to the house. With this purchase, we were now pretty well financially strapped for payments. Meaning we were maxed out. Things needed to click pretty good in order to keep things rolling. But I was not worried. I knew business, and I knew what I needed to do to bring in even more money to get on top of our payments. And about that time was when I left for Fresh Start and life would never be the same for us ever again. Of course, I thought I would be back with business as soon as I had found some help for myself. That didn't happen. At least not in the way I expected.

I came to Fresh Start on the bottom part of 2006 which was just before the economy crashed. In 2008, the whole economy crashed, and the value of housing market absolutely fell out. Just seconds before the economy crashed in 2008, we were fortunate enough to sell the $500,000 property, but for a little less than what we had just got done paying for it. It was sold soon after I'd went to Fresh Start. I was so thankful that we got to sell that property rather than have the bank take it over. But the other house we had was nothing that fancy, just a regular Florida home; we lost it to the bank during this housing market crash. We were at Fresh Start, our produce business had been sold, and there was nobody out there to keep the payments going. It was a shame to us in any way you looked at it, but there was just simply nothing I could do about it. Nothing. I felt totally helpless. I was not about to walk away from Fresh Start until I felt my life was made right with God. That walk went much longer than I ever expected it to be. My life with God and my family came first before business. This earthly stuff was just earthly stuff. It wasn't easy, but I knew what was best for me. Before we let the house go back to the bank, a couple of the men in our church back home in Florida who were looking over our assets were nice enough to fly up here to Indiana to help us make the right decision with that property, and we decided the best thing we could do was let it go back to the bank because it might be a while before we get done with the program. Somebody needed to make payments, and that was not going to happen with me not having a job to bring in revenue.

So here we were, starting out with no money to our name, only two vehicles, the clothes on our back, and were looking for a place to rent here in Daviess County, Indiana. Where do we start? This was an exciting time for us and, at the very same time, very frightening. We depended on Fresh Start for food and a place to live at for the last two years of a very difficult time in our lives. Now we were about to step out in the real world and start all over on our very own again.

By the time we graduated from Fresh Start, our oldest daughter already had a job, and she wasn't interested to pull away from that. Also, by now, the children all felt very much at home in Daviess County with the church and the children their age group around here. As parents, Fresh Start Chapel felt like home to us. The people. Everyone. So we decided to stay around here for the time being.

This steel manufacturing place was a total new experience for me, working with steel. I was a wood-worker by trade, not steel. When I applied for a job at this place, I thought I was only going to be their driver to run to and fro on the road. I had absolutely no desire to work with steel. I had heard through the grapevine that Graber Steel was looking for some-one as a driver, and I thought that sounded like a good way to get some revenue started coming in. But instead, they started me out as a welder for the time being. Beings most of the employees were Amish, I was provided with a work van, and I'd go around picking up workers in the early morning hours and then take them back home in the evenings again. Getting to learn the trade in the steel manufacturing end will be an experience I will be forever grateful for also. I learned the tricks of working with steel like I never knew before. Eventually, I did more and more road trips for the business, which was more my cup of tea, but welding was not as bad as I thought it might be at first. I enjoyed getting out of the shop and doing something else for a spell, doing road run errands.

After four years with Graber Steel, it was time for me to move on. I longed more than ever to go back on my own once again. To be my own boss again. Things just seemed to go better for me that way.

By now, my wife was pretty much doing full-time taxi work in the community, doing short runs and long-distance runs with our van she had purchased for just that. Occasionally, I would do a long-distance run over the weekend as well. Now and then, I would take runs during the week, and it paid pretty well. I really enjoyed doing long-distance runs. I always enjoyed traveling and sight-seeing. But these runs seemed to really interfere with my job at Graber Steel at times, and it did not go down very well with my boss. Especially when I would take runs during the week. Now I must say though that I could not have asked for a better boss, and so this made it very tough and very uncomfortable and really hard for me to tell him I had plans to quit working for his company. For the most part, I did like my job there at Graber Steel other than I was having this very difficult situation with a coworker that I just could not go on working under these circumstances. It was like this lemon had been poured out all over the floor, and I could not make lemonade with it. I had been dealing with this for some time already, and whenever I talked to the boss about it, he and his boys always seemed to stick up for the other fella since he had been with them longer than I had been and so it didn't make any difference what I thought on the matter. This fella had not only been on the job longer than I, he was also their biggest buddy. And so it was just not going to work out for me to stay any longer. He would do anything to make me feel uncomfortable whenever he could. Or so it seemed to me. The time came for me to go. It really interfered with my work and just totally took the fun out of my work there.

I still had this thing in the back of my mind about having a country store again, something like our little store we had back in Sarasota, Florida.

So here again, my mind was once again just blown as to how God opened all these doors for us as we pursued the possibly to open our little dream store. There was really no question as what we should do next. Everything just seemed to fall in place for us. We did go through a tough spell financially once again to get to where we wanted to get to. But if you want to see where God took us from here, you must keep on reading. It will blow your mind. It was totally amazing. Through prayer and seeking direction from the Lord, God worked a miracle we never thought possible. I did not see all this coming our way nor was it even something I was working toward, but God knew my desire since I was a little Amish boy back in Ohio. Now fifteen years after graduating from Fresh Start, here I am, the owner of six charter buses and they are all paid for. Now, you figure that one out. You can't tell me God isn't good, *all the time*. Even in the times that seem tough. But before I got into the charter bus business, I need to tell you how we got to this point of owning a bus company. I never thought I would get to this part in my life. Thought it would always remain just a dream.

Going back to the time I quit Graber Steel and Fab and taking this leap of faith, trusting things would work out for us. So I located this little hole-in-the-wall store in Loogootee, Indiana (pronounced "La-go-tee"). Not really the ideal place, but it would have to do to get me started. And that is just exactly what it did, it got us going to where we are today. I had a hard time finding a location that seemed suitable for what I really wanted for a small store selling wood crafts, bulk foods, and prepackaged meats and cheeses. I even had a little corner in the back of this one room where I could set up a few woodworking tools and make crafts right there in the back of the store while it was not busy with customers out front. This little room there in the back even had about half of the floor where it wasn't concrete. This was down-town Loogootee where you would have thought everything should be a little more upscale, right? This was not a very large town, but we were on a busy road, and that surely meant something. Dirt floor in the back room. Nothing fancy. Now, the main part of the store had just been newly remodeled. New carpet. New walls. It was a perfect little hole-in-the-wall store to start in.

About the time I had this store secured, meaning I paid my deposit and the first month of rent and was ready to go, I went and put in my two-week notice of quitting Graber Steel. This was not easy for me to do. And it was not without lots of mixed feelings and emotions. I was questioning myself whether I was doing the right thing or not. I knew in my heart what I wanted. But the enemy likes to play tricks with your mind, and sometimes, it is hard to know what is right or what is wrong in situations like this. Would we be able to make it financially on our own like this, without the biweekly paycheck I was getting from Graber Steel? If we were going to do this, I was going to have to take this leap in faith that God would also provide for us. Malinda was still doing regular taxi work with her little twelve-passenger Chevy van we now had. This in itself was a good feeling because it brought in pretty good money in case the little store would be a total flop. There was always this possibility that I could do some of her runs and she could watch the store if she so preferred.

After we opened the little store for business, it did happen more often than we thought it would. I'd do the runs and she'd watch the store. The little store started out extremely slow for business. We didn't do any advertising. Just word of mouth and a small homemade sign out on the front sidewalks. We only had a verbal agreement on the rental for this store, but the owner of the building liked for us to stay at least a year if we could. But after only five months in this little store, business had not picked up at all. It was getting very depressing and boring for the person waiting behind the counter for customers. In fact, I think rather than it starting to pick up a customer base, it slowed down from when we first opened up.

This was not going to work out. What we had in our little store was just absolutely not bringing in repeat customers for some reason. The location probably had a huge effect for this. I'm not sure what all played in with this, except it was just not working out at all. And I had no intentions of going back to Graber Steel where I had just come from. It was time to switch gears and to switch pretty fast. So I pretty much went full-time hauling for the Amish, doing taxi work, and Malinda stayed at the store for the time being. The store was not even making enough to cover the monthly rent, which of course meant the rest of the rent money had to come from somewhere else. Taxi money, that's where. That could only work for so long and something else would need to be done eventually. The little store was simply taking us for a slow downward spiral. But I was not ready to hang it up just yet. There *had* to be something we could do to start bringing in customers. Surely! There just had to be. One thing was for certain, though, our location was probably 75 percent of the problem. We had no parking lot for customers. People had to park along the street in front of the store, and there was not even much room for that. So here I was, scratching my head day in and day out, figuring out how to make this thing work. It got so slow, that it was downright boring to sit there in that store, waiting and hoping for customers all day long. I couldn't even enjoy myself working on any projects back there in the other little room no more, it was so boring, depressing. The excitement was just not there anymore; business was too slow. Now, if customers just rolled in that door and everybody was just thrilled with the little store and they just loved our items and things just flew off the shelves like hot-cakes, this would have given anyone the boost and excitement that any store owner desired. But it was quite the opposite. Malinda also got so bored sitting all day at this little store, and our customer base was so terribly low that she had rather go on van runs than to sit there bored all day long, waiting on customers. So here I was, back in the store. Malinda was back out on the road. But the Lord knew what he was doing. On this one particular day, I was again out back on the dirt floor in the back room, cutting out small crafts out of wood on my little scroll saw, when suddenly, I just got this real heavy urge down in my heart to cry out to God for help. Where had my prayer time gone to anyway? Something inside of me told me it was time to do something different. I'm sure God heard my groanings from within, and He knew my needs and my desires, and I don't think my desires were wrong. But God wanted me to ask. Not just wait. Ask, and it shall be given to you. I was extremely bored and depressed that my little store was not doing what I thought it should. I dropped what I was doing, which wasn't hard to do, for it was too slow to be excited about anything right then. I went out front, got behind the counter where I should have been taking care of customers, and stared out the front window. There was a ton of traffic going by. In fact, our storefront was right next to the main highway in the middle of town, and it was pretty noisy at times with all that traffic, but no one bothered to stop. One time, I just verbally cried out to God for help. If this store was not a good idea, if this store was not meant to be, then I prayed God would give me a sign. That God would send something else my way. That I would be okay within myself to shut down this store and do something else if God wants me to. I didn't know what that would be, but I was ready for whatever it was that God would send my way. I asked that if God was closing the doors for this store, that He would open another door for us *somewhere*. In the back of my mind, this was sort of hard to ask for because I felt it so plain in my heart that I was making the right move from Graber Steel to this store at the time. If that was the right move, then why is it not working out? I was a little more than puzzled here. I was a bit frustrated as well. But I cried out to God to open another door, because it felt for certain that the doors were closing in on us right here. Right after I had prayed, I went back to cutting out a few more things on my little scroll saw, feeling somewhat a little relief in my heavy heart. Normally, I would have really enjoyed my woodworking, but right now, it was not much fun. It was too boring and lonely. But here is where this story becomes almost too good to be true. God was listening. I was nearly blown away what happened next. Literally. Well almost. That very same afternoon, after I had cried out to the Lord in prayer, as I was back there cutting out crafts, still feeling down and bored, still depressed, I heard the front door open. A customer? A customer just walked in. Or so I thought. The man had rich, dark, black hair and he was dressed up like a real salesman and he had this real deep rough voice that carried throughout the whole store. His voice carried so deep that I wished for him to lower his voice so our neighbors across the wall next door wouldn't hear our conversation. Seriously!

I did not know this man from Adam. He told the same about me. I thought I had a customer that would surely make a sale for me, but it was quite different. He had no intentions of buying anything. He leaned in over my counter there and started telling me how he was driving by here and just so happened to see our little sign in the door. He told me he had actually driven on by, but something told him he needs to turn around and go back there and talk to the person inside that store. So that is why he was here. He introduced himself as Tim Carico.

"I know you don't know me from Adam, but I own Amish Kountry Korner up there on Highway 50 in Washington, up the road about twelve miles. I just stopped in to see if you would be interested in buying me out?"

I held my breath for a few seconds before I could speak. I knew *exactly* where he was referring to, and it was *all* I could do to not scream out *loud,* at the top of my lungs, "Yes, I want that store." I pretended to not be overly excited, and I asked several more questions about the store. Before he left, I told him that

I was definitely interested, but our biggest problem would be the money. I told him I was sure he wanted way more money than I had, and we had absolutely no credit to our name for a loan. I told him that. (I was remembering our bad credit to our name back in Florida with our house going back to the bank. Our credit was zero zip zap at its best, but of course, I didn't relate this with him.) Just graduated from Fresh Start. We had absolutely no credit to our name when you mentioned money or a bank. That would be our biggest problem, I told him. Before he left, he laid down a piece of paper on the counter with his name and phone number and told me to give him a call, that he was sure we could make it happen somehow. He opened the front door and walked out. I'm sure he probably didn't expect to ever hear from me ever again. I could almost not call Malinda quick enough to tell her what had just happened. I was in absolute disbelief. Did this actually just happen?

Chapter 13

Amish Kountry Korner

Back when I was still in the Fresh Start Program, we would drive by this unique little country store named Amish Kountry Korner several times a week, every Sunday to church and every Wednesday evenings for prayer meeting. I always had my eye on this little country store. Not in my wildest dreams would I ever had the nerve to ask the owner if he ever thought about selling that little store. Never thought I would even had the slightest chance at it.

So here, the very day, within just an hour or so of me crying out to God, He answered my prayer. Talk about having my faith strengthened once again, for real. My excitement was once again on cloud nine, and I felt like there might still be hope after all. Was there still light at the end of this tunnel? I could hardly contain my excitement until I had to remind myself that we would surely come up against a solid brick wall once the man gave me the price of the store. I was just not sure how we would cross that hurdle. Guess by now I should have learned to trust the Lord to take care of everything. This was a well-established country store that carried bulk foods, a full line of meat and cheeses and a deli, carry-out deli sandwiches, crafts, and a whole lot more. This little store was loaded. The only way I could see that I'd even had the slightest chance at this store was by a miracle. Yes, a true miracle. There was no other way. Malinda and I stopped by that little store one day that very next week to check it out. I had very seldom been inside of the store, maybe once or twice. The Mennonite lady in the store showed us around. We told her what we were there for. She was the only person working there, and she showed us all around the little place. One thing I wasn't so sure about was the business side of making sandwiches. I wasn't looking for a restaurant. Making sandwiches in this little country store somewhat reminded me of a restaurant attached to the bulk-food side of the store. But I was not going to let this stop me from buying it if it was within our reach. I wasn't so sure about slapping meat and cheese between two pieces of bread, squirting mayonnaise all over it, and putting the rest of the fixin's on that sandwich, and telling the customer, "There ya go. Appreciate it, have a good day." That didn't really appeal to me.

Something like a week later, I decided I needed to call the guy back before he goes and sells the store to someone else out from under me. It still felt like a far reach for me, but I knew God loves to work miracles in our lives, and I shouldn't just give up on it this quick. After all, He answered my cry that very day, why should I not trust Him all the way? Could He not provide a way for us to buy the store, if He sent the man to my store that day when I was about to give up? I also figured this man never expected to hear from me again after that day he had stopped in to talk to me. So when I called him, he immediately wanted to set up a meeting with him and his partner, another fella who lived about three hours away. He wondered when we could do that. This made me feel about, this small. Yes, this small. Me, sit down with this high-class businessman and his partner in business? I felt pretty small. So if he was in with another person, how was I ever to buy these guys out? This seemed pretty far out for me. I was not interested in going into a business with another partner, and the price surely would be far over our head at this rate, I thought. Just the thought of it nearly gave me the heebie-jeebies. I knew deep down in my heart, I really wanted this store. It was right here at the tips of my fingers, and all I needed was the money to make it happen. Money that I probably didn't have. Or even more than money, I needed a miracle from God if we were to have this store. And faith. Lots of faith. There is no mountain that God cannot move. So if he can move mountains, then he could make this work out for us too. Do I have that kind of faith in God?

We set up a meeting which was set up to be right there at the store itself. The two men sat right there at a round table in the middle of the room among merchandise to be sold in this little room to the side. The store was divided out in different rooms, each room carrying different types of items for sale throughout the store.

Malinda and I sat on the opposite side of the table. I felt pretty much out of place to be sitting with these high-profile men to negotiate a price for this store when in reality, it seemed pretty far-fetched from me. Or so I thought. But after some talk, these men went right to the point of the price they were looking at. They probably decided it was not worth the time to waste a whole lot of time here hee-hawing around the bush with this Mennonite couple who had no clue if we had it in us to pull this one off or not. These two men had no Amish or Mennonite background. They were town men at their best, well sort of. I suppose they thought, either these folks will have the money to do the deal or they don't. So let's get right to business. And they did. They got right to the price. I was once again about blown away when I heard the price. The price was actually within our reach, I thought. I could hardly believe it. My cup was running over with joy within. Surely, we could make this happen, I thought. And we did, we made the deal and took over the store. Now, this was not the *only* miracle in this purchase. There was more. God did a lot more than just answer my prayer to open another door. This was about right the time when a huge project was about to begin within a mile from this little store. That project would last a couple years in itself. Perfect timing for us to purchase this little store while we had this huge interstate go in within a mile from us and all these out of state workers in the area. The project I'm referring to was that of a four-lane interstate I-69 was coming right through our town of Washington, Indiana, and go right through the Amish community of Daviess County, Indiana. These workers started coming to our store for deli sandwiches, and we offered cold drinks, fountain drinks, chips, ice cream and baked goods along with them. For these workers, this was a whole lot better deal to them than it was to run in town and get any fast-food meal and a whole lot healthier food too. They just loved it. We got hundreds of compliments from these guys. With this huge interstate project going on for the next couple of years, this gave us such an immediately boost in business that in no time we paid off the store and we did very well with it.

Sandwiches? It didn't take me long to figure out this, along with the cheese and meat deli, was where the money was to be made at. And it was fun. This store was mainly known for its bulk foods and hard-to-find spices and such. This new interstate going in just a mile up the road quickly made this place into a sandwich and lunch stop for many of the workers. And it wasn't long when the whole neighborhood was coming by to get sandwiches for lunch.

Now looking back, what I see is this. Had I not started up this little store in Loogootee, Indiana, first, this Tim Carico guy would never have met me in the first place and I'd never got Amish Kountry Korner, a store I had my eyes on for several years already. God *answered* my prayer in that little store back in Loogootee, the very day I had asked, when I was at my wits' end working back there on that little dirt floor, bored and lonely, not knowing which way to turn no more. And I knew what I needed to do. I needed to turn my heart to God and pray. I couldn't do this on my own. That little hole-in-the-wall store was not working out.

Now after a year or so with Amish Kountry Korner, we had tripled our customer base. We added a whole lot more inventory to the store than what was originally there when we took over, including hard-to-find items, like in the line of herbs and spices, candies, and bulk-food items. This store truly was a dream store come true for me. I had to slow down the van runs that I was doing in the community. We hired a couple workers, plus Malinda and I were in there full-time and also our daughter Loretta. Even though I enjoyed working in the store, I also still had several other interests that I still enjoyed very much. I still enjoyed my little woodworking shop and so I still made crafts for the store and sold a lot of it. After owning and running the store for nearly four years, Malinda suddenly came down flat on her back, meaning her back was giving her major problems. Her back had been bothering her some time

177

already but not to this extent. This one came on her very suddenly, and one morning, she simply could not walk anymore and was in a lot of pain. She was the backbone of this busy little store. We had several employees, and they were a huge help in the store, but without Malinda in there working alongside of them, things just didn't seem to roll as smoothly. If for nothing else, we needed Malinda in there for the customers' sake. They just loved to stop by and chat with her. It truly did build up our relationship with our customers and they loved it. Of course, Malinda did much more than just talk with customers. She truly was the backbone of this business. I, for myself, really enjoyed the business part of the store, and at the same time, I was still out on the road quite a bit, not so much with van runs anymore, but I was doing bus runs by now. I got a big thrill out of having Amish Kountry Korner, but at the same time, I still liked my outside work just the same. If we could had employees who had the same vision and force toward the store as we had, allowing Malinda to have days off, this would have been great. But it just didn't work out that way. Hardly ever does. Sometime during these four years, while we had Amish Kountry Korner, I had bought my very first charter bus. This was something I dreamed about since I was a little Amish boy back home in Ohio. I *always* wanted to drive a big bus, but I never expected it to become a reality for me ever. God has shown Himself stronger and more powerful than I could have ever imagined in this. So here I was, the bus business was starting to pick up, and I wanted to see where that business would take us. And here at almost the very same time, suddenly, Malinda gets down flat on her back, unable to work. The demand of the store was booming faster than the employees could keep up. Either Malinda or I or both needed to be in the store at all times to keep the flow going smoothly. As much as I enjoyed the store myself, my main interest probably wasn't out front with the customers. I would rather stay behind the scene, working in the back somewhere. Working back in the kitchen area. Our daughter Loretta did a fantastic job out front, taking the customers' money, and they just loved it. She did a good job out front, but she commented how she had also rather stayed in the back. But I needed a person like her out front. Customers thoroughly enjoyed seeing and chatting with our children and having them being involved in the business. Many were repeat customers, and they got very attached to our children working in there. I had absolutely no intentions of ever getting rid of the store even while the charter bus business was keeping me on the road a whole lot more than I ever expected. When I started out with the bus business, I never thought Daviess County Amish community would be large enough to make the bus business a full-time business. In other words, I didn't expect to stay busy. At this time, the store did me a lot of good; it was a dream come true for me. I thought it would be our main business for many years to come. At the same time, I never expected the bus business to ever grow into more than just the one bus that I had. Didn't even expect to keep the one bus busy on the road. When I bought the bus, my initial thought was if I couldn't keep it busy, at least I got to drive a big bus like I always dreamed of doing, and then I will just sell it again. When I was out on the road, I was always calling Malinda, asking how business was at the store. It always felt good to hear that the store was booming. It brought lots of excitement and a thrill to me even while I was out on the road. I loved the business. But when Malinda came down on her back and wasn't able to work anymore and we were facing a hard time knowing what to do, it became very difficult for us. She was facing the possibility of having to do surgery on her back. I was between a rock and a hard spot, literally. Some of our older children thought we needed to sell the store immediately, that we could not continue on like this with neither Malinda nor I in the store. They kept telling me that I could not continue with both the store and the charter bus business at the same time. We didn't have much time to figure out what we needed to do. Malinda was in bad shape with her back, and we needed to do something very soon.

When Mom gets down, the children get pretty excited. When Dad gets down, nobody gets excited.

Wonder if anybody else had this experience already, LOL.

I didn't have time to find a good manager to run the store, which we should have had in place I suppose. We were trying to manage everything ourselves, and now here all at once, we found us in a difficult spot and things needed to happen right now or we could not move forward in either of our businesses. It was a very, *very* unpleasant feeling. I did not want to sell the store nor did I want to sell the bus, but the children were pushing for one or the other to go. This absolutely tore me at my heart. It felt like a giant took both of his hands to my chest and just ripped me apart. Both businesses probably meant the same much to me. Both were making good money, so it wasn't like, well, let's get rid of this one because this one over here is really the main one bringing in the money. It was truly a very, *very* difficult decision for me. I had a passion for both. For one, this store was something I had an eye on for the whole time I was at Fresh Start, not thinking I would ever had a chance at it. And then with a miracle, it happened. It was a God miracle. I didn't even have to go look for it. The fella walked right through my door, asking me if I wanted to buy him out, right after I had just finished praying an hour earlier. It was mine. How was this supposed to make me feel? I wasn't sure, but I needed to trust in the Lord through the good and the bad. I enjoyed the retail side of a store very much ever since I was a teen in my dad's furniture shop growing up. The bus business was something I dreamed of as a teen working in my dad's furniture shop. While I had the gasoline motor purring at a high RPM and the wood planer planing board after board, the sound of it always reminded me of the sound of the old Greyhound buses as we used to ride them. I would often pretend to be driving a bus while planing boards. Not that I thought I would ever in my life drive a bus, but little boys do dream.

The charter bus business was something I had just recently gotten into, and what really motivated me to actually get a charter bus in the first place was to start doing regular runs to Sarasota, Florida, in the winter months out of Daviess County, Indiana. Soon after I bought the bus, I put together a plan and a schedule for the Sarasota run and got brochures printed and I even advertised in the local Amish community paper. And now I was in between this rock and a hard place, and I felt horrible to pull out of it now. I already had folks all excited about having a regular bus run to Sarasota, Florida, during the winter months. At the very same time that I had some people excited about the Florida runs, I also had several Amish men tell me straight in my face that it would *never* work. One Amish guy in the community looked me straight in my face, lowered his tone of voice, and said, "Nealie, it will never work. It will never work. You will never have enough people to go every week to make it work."

And this was an older fella from the community who was fairly much looked up to, an Amish businessman himself. That was not what I wanted to hear. Neither was it what I needed to hear. So I just simply told him how I felt, and that was this, that if I never try it, I will never know. He looked at me again with those same gleaming eyes, "But, Nealie, it'll take you down financially," looking very concerned for my sake.

Again, I told him I was prepared for that possibility. It could be a big flop. That was very possible. I had saved up enough money during the summer to cover me for the weekly runs this winter, *even* if it meant it was going to be a very slow, unprofitable season for me. In fact, I was bracing myself for just that. I really had no idea if this was going to work or not, but one thing I did know was that a lot of Daviess County people went to Florida during the winter. Why not ride the bus? We would put together the schedule, the drivers, and we would do the driving. All the folks needed to do was call and reserve their seat and leave the driving to us. How could it get any better than this? I was determined to try it for at least one winter. Something on the inside of me said it would work. If it worked, great. If it didn't, well, then I would know, and I'd have to hang it up. But this was my main motivation for getting into the bus business, to do winter Florida runs, and I was going to do it at least one winter. The Amish fella looked at me one more time and he asked, "But what if there was *only one person* scheduled to go, what will you do then? You cannot run that way."

I said, "If we have one person that bought a ticket to go, the bus will be running."

He looked at me with a very, *very* concerned look on his face, and he slapped his horse with his leather driving lines and he went on his way. I know he meant it for the best for me. He was a huge businessman of Daviess County, a man well-known in the community, but he definitely did not have the same vision I had. I think he would have been all for it, but he could not envision it being profitable for me and he knew the buses definitely do not run for cheap. They take a lot of fuel. A lot of maintenance and a lot of upkeep.

That first winter we had one run that we had nobody going southbound and only one person riding back north with us. That was the worse week we had that winter, and of course, that run wasn't profitable. In fact, we lost money, but we did not let the person down or let her fend for herself to find a way home. We ran. Our bus was there for her. We already had this one ticket sold; therefore, we knew we needed to run for her. Otherwise, if we had no tickets sold for that particular week, we would not have run that week. At the end of that season, we knew it was a success, and I knew we had started a good thing. We started by running the last week of October and ran every other week through November. Starting in December, we ran every week up until the second week into April.

While writing this chapter, we have now run every winter since, and we are into our ninth season. These Florida runs have proven to be one of my most favorite runs we do with these buses.

Going back to the store again. The rock and the hard spot I was in. Not a good feeling. What do I do with the store? I would've preferred more time to sort this thing out and make this all work out yet. The store, it was a part of me. It was my heartbeat. By now, I was too busy on the road with bus runs, and it was clear to me I couldn't be both in the store and on the road at the same time. There was only one of me. Our children simply did not have enough interest in the store to keep it going. I didn't have time to wait this thing out until I could find a really good person to manage the store. A decision had to be made quickly. The store was far too busy to not have enough employees present every day.

Up until now, it seemed I was never able to hang on to a business of mine for very long until I needed to move on to something else. There always seemed to be a stumbling block or something that came along and I needed to change something. First off, I thought I'd never be anything but a lawn furniture builder. That lasted until everyone in our area was moving out of Palmer Square area, and we moved to Florida and joined the Beachy Amish Mennonite church. It wasn't long after we had moved that the whole Amish settlement dissolved and there was no one left in that area no more. Palmer Square area was home to me ever since I was two years old. I never thought I would ever move from that area. Even more so, I never thought I would see the day that my dad would move out of that area. My dad had a lawn furniture business going there that boomed from the day he started it. Even more than that, it was home to all of us. But a few Amish families clapped their hands together, and everybody scattered every which way like a flock of blackbirds. Boom, they were gone and there was no looking back.

First: after Malinda and I got married, I had started up my own lawn furniture business. I always dreamed of having a huge lawn furniture business. I wanted a large retail store to go along with it. It was just something I longed for and wanted to have. And then it wasn't long when we realized we needed a change of direction in our life. At the same time that everybody was moving out of this area, we had gotten ourselves tangled up in with wrong friends that enjoyed partying. We too enjoyed the party life at the time, but we realized it was getting us nowhere in life but in a downward spiral. It was just not our calling in life. So we decided the best way to do this was to simply move completely out of the area. Now, I must say, I do not hate our friends, Larry and Tina. They have souls just like we do. They needed friends, and we needed friends. I also didn't know the Lord as my Lord and Savior at the time, so who is to blame? Maybe it would be more accurate to say we were both in the wrong.

Looking back now, we can see how the Lord was directing us all along the way, which we are forever grateful for. But unfortunately, there went my dream for my lawn furniture business.

Second: after our move to Florida, I thought I would continue with my lawn furniture business, but that was not going to happen either. So instead, I worked for Sutter's Egg Farm as farm manager for five years until we went on our own and got into a completely different direction in business, but still in retail, selling produce and food products. After we had started this business, I realized this was something I can enjoy and we can grow our business in. I could see myself be in this for the long haul. I thought I had finally found the business that we would have for a long, *long* time. But the good Lord had other plans again. As quickly as I had started it, after four years, He took everything away from me again. Just that quick, it was gone. If one is not living for God, He will not be able to bless the business and one will not prosper forever. I was asked by our ministers to go get help at Fresh Start and get counseling to understand the nature of how God looks at sin. Sin has consequences. It affected my family, my business, and everything we had going for ourselves.

Third: so now here we were again, needing to make a decision in my business between the little country store we had or my charter bus business. As I looked at the charter bus business and the store side of the business, I knew I had something good going with the charter bus business. Without a store manager in place, this was going to be difficult to keep the store going. My wife had been managing the store since I have been on the road a lot with the buses, and now she was down on her back. She could no longer work in the store at this point, and our girls demanded she no longer work in the store. At the moment though, we had Mary Ellen Miller working in the store who had just moved up from Sarasota, Florida, recently along with her husband Wilmer. So we offered the store to them, and they bought it from us. I struggled for a long time, along with lots of mixed feelings whether I made the right choice in selling that store. That store right there had been very good to us. It made us money. It was a food-related store. People will always need food. People will always need to eat. On the other hand, if the economy got tight financially, people might not travel as much, and that could affect the charter bus business. Then what would I do? Those were options that I was trying to weigh out in my mind. I wanted to trust the Lord that it was not my will but His; He knew what was best for us.

We still lived right next door to the store for a while longer after we'd sold it, on the same lot. In the meantime, I bought three acres of land in Montgomery, Indiana, just three miles down the road from where we sold the store. This property only had one lonely building on it, and it was not in real good shape. It wasn't good enough for us to live in as a house and not big enough to pull my bus into to work on. It was built a pole barn style, but was somewhat insulated. Many of the posts were rotted off at floor level on the concrete. Not sure what kept the wind from blowing the whole building over on its side. Possibly the hill and trees to the west side of us were a big wind block for the building. But then sometimes, those older buildings seem to just stand the test of time.

Before we got moved out of the house next door to the store there, I had bought my second bus already. This was primarily for the sake of having a second bus available so I could have the one bus in the shop if needed and still have one available for the runs that were on schedule. Many times, I really needed to have the one bus in the shop getting work done on it, but because of all the runs scheduled, it made it difficult to keep up with maintenance. But before I even had that second bus at home, it was already booked out, which meant both buses were going to be out over the same time. In many ways, this was a huge blessing to be this busy, but now, I was back to square one. I couldn't get my maintenance done as I had planned. And it continued this way. Soon, I bought my third bus. This one was a fifty-six-passenger coach and the newer style bus. Immediately, this one also was being booked out. More drivers were needed which continues to be a real struggle for us today yet. Being I was still on the road a lot myself, I was not hiring full-time drivers, only part-time drivers. This made it difficult many times to have enough drivers to fill all the runs we had booked. Our business continued to grow, and we are currently up to six buses and they are all paid for. This has proven to be a huge blessing for us, to not be in debt with our bus business. If I would have bought these buses with a loan and I had payments to make, above all the ridiculous amounts of high maintenance that goes with operating these buses, I'd have a difficult time making it, if not even lost the business by now. It took an awful lot of patience to grow as we did to wait until I had the money in the bank before I bought my next bus. When I look back over the years we've been in business and we now have six coaches and they are all paid for, in these short years after graduating from Fresh Start, starting out with nothing and now to this, it still blows my mind. God has been good to us, and for that, we are grateful. We've come much farther then I could have ever dreamed of being at this point. If someone had told me when I graduated, that in fifteen years from now, you will own six charter buses and they will all be paid for, I would probably have told you that that was impossible.

I'm here to tell you, never underestimate God's power and his wonderful mercies that are new every day.

I have become a believer that if you change from the old person that you once were to living a new life for God and you believe in the Lord Jesus Christ and you do all your work as unto the Him, He will bless you beyond what you can imagine. Yes, I will admit, there are days I still get discouraged when things don't want to go the way I think they ought to go. If you live in that moment for too long, it's scary, because then, I feel like throwing in the towel and go back to my younger years and party it away again. I know deep in my heart that this is not what I want. I have to stop myself and remember where I came from just a few short years ago. I graduated from Fresh Start with no money in the bank. Pretty much just the clothes on our backs. One vehicle. Didn't own a home. Seven hungry children to feed. Had very little to our name. We were truly starting out with a fresh start. Life looked pretty dim at the time. But we had our hearts washed white as snow, and we knew we had the Lord Jesus in our hearts. We were set to start out with a fresh new start in life.

Chapter 14

The House

My beloved little country store has been sold to Wilmer and Mary Ellen Miller. This is not what I wanted to do at all. It hurt. It hurt deeply. At the same moment, it seemed like it was the only option I had at the time. Malinda, my dear wife, was facing back surgery. Her back had just very suddenly given out. Her back had been giving her problems for some time already, but she pretty much had kept it to herself and no one knew it was really that bad.

So this meant we would be moving again here real soon. Since there was no house on our three-acre property yet that we had just recently bought, we would be moving in a rental house for a while. The property worked perfectly to park our buses there, and the little old building came in handy for my little woodworking shop and keep all my tools in to work on my buses for the time being. But it became a real drag for me to run from our rental house to the bus terminal numerous times in a day. This got old very quick, but until we got our new house built there, we had no other option. I had to run back and forth.

The bus business continued to grow and was doing quite well for us. I look back now and am absolutely amazed as to how I get to have these big charter buses as my business, especially when I remember how I grew up as a little Amish boy, only going through the eighth grade in school, the highest of school education that I ever studied. My schooling? Hands-on, buddy. Hands-on, the best schooling one can attain, if you ask me. A lot of the high schooling is downright garbage. A lot of the stuff you learn in there are things you will probably never ever use again in your entire lifetime after you graduate high school. If you are pursuing to become a doctor, then I understand you will need to do extra studying. If you plan to become a lawyer, you'll need extra studying. Study according what your goals are in life. Don't waste your time on garbage that you will never use in your entire lifetime ever again. It is a simple waste of your time, and you are robbing time away from helping your parents, hands-on training. You will never get better training than hands-on. If you want to become a diesel truck mechanic, go to a diesel truck college and learn hands-on where they tear the complete engine down piece by piece and you put it back together again, piece by piece. Now you actually understand how this engine actually runs and operates.

I always loved business. You may get tired of reading this in my story here, but by now, you know that owning my own little furniture store is something I always longed for when I would envision my future growing up. That was my goal in life. So I grew up in my dad's lawn furniture business. This is where I picked up the interest of business and woodworking. I took care of my dad's lawn furniture business as a young teenager. Got married and thought I would have a lifelong business in lawn furniture just like my dad did. Several years into our marriage, life started taking a different shape for us as we got into the partying with a young local couple as you've read earlier on in my story. When we had enough of that, we thought we would just quit and be normal again, right? Well, it wasn't that easy. I look back now and see how God might have been trying to get our attention earlier on, but we were too naïve to understand, I guess. I guess it took more to get my attention to understand what God's plans was for us. Quite frankly, I'm not sure I even knew there was such a thing as God having a plan for every soul. I assumed it meant to do the walk and stay in the walk of the Amish, and I'd make it to heaven. So there was this big void in my life that I was trying to fill on my own. Remember one thing, God's calling for you might be different than it was for me. But when God calls you, listen and follow.

When our friends started coming back around again, we of course couldn't tell them no, and we got tangled right back into the partying again, barhopping, and the like. So later on, we both felt like God was asking us to move to Florida, as I explained earlier on when one day out of nowhere, I got this urgent feeling within that we need to move to Florida. That evening, after Malinda came home from her day job she had in town, *which was actually forbidden by the Amish rules,* she had that very same feeling to share with me. But before she came home, my urge was so high, I could hardly wait to tell her about the feeling I had that day. Remember, these were the days before cell phones were invented. I couldn't just up and call or text her like we do today. Well, lo and behold, she was feeling the very same thing that I was that day while she was at work. We had not even discussed this beforehand. After we talked about it briefly, she said, "Let's go."

We made some real fast moves, had an auction, and we moved to Florida. We lived in Sarasota for about a year and hardly attended any church at all. We were too timid. Didn't know many people, but we lived right there in the middle of Pinecraft. Made new friends every day but still didn't attend church anywhere. Didn't even really feel like attending church at the time. In a way, you might think, we were just plain downright bad people. I'm not sure I would agree with you. I might admit we were slow learners. You have to remember where we came from. We didn't know just where life was going to take us just yet. We were taking our time, I guess. I believe God knew exactly what He was doing, and He knew exactly what it took to get us where He wanted us, so He could use us in the future to further His kingdom. About a year into living in Sarasota, a friend of ours thought we should try go to Sunnyside Mennonite Church for church to see if we would like that. So whew, finally got up enough courage to go. We had no idea how a Mennonite church operates. We were scared. Afraid. But we went anyway. That day, Sunnyside Church was having communion service and Lester Gingerich, the bishop, had the message, and I was very touched with the message that day. I had never heard such a powerful spirit-filled message in my entire life that I'm aware of. Everything made sense to me. I could hear God's voice. God was on the move. I could feel it within. When we left church that day, on our way back home, I asked Malinda what she thought of church or the message. I don't remember her response, but when she asked me what I thought of it, I told her, "This is the church we will be attending."

I had never heard someone preach with such sincerity and truth to where I was so touched with the message. The message was not all about the Ordnung of church and its rules. The message was on the suffering of Christ and what it meant to me. Lester preached the true message of salvation that day. See, I was brought up in a church where they preached so much on church rules. You go against church rules you're going to hell. I knew of heaven and hell because of how it was preached, but I didn't know God. Oh yes, I knew there was a God, but I did not have a true relationship with Jesus Christ.

We continued attending Sunnyside and eventually ended up becoming members at the church.

But I would still need to someday come clean from that baggage I had been carrying around for a long time that I did not know how to shake on my own. It wasn't real long when Bill Yoder, who also attended that church, had asked me to come work for him at Sutter's. While I was employed there, Bill was ordained minister there at Sunnyside Mennonite Church. And then of course, later on, we started up our little store there in Venice, just south of Sarasota, selling produce. It was there when I would be going to Fresh Start to take care of the sin baggage that I had carried with me from all the way back from the time we had left Ohio, and I was just not strong enough on my own to shake it off. I couldn't find true repentance. I needed help to do that. I would tell myself, *This is it, I will sin no more.* But the next day was a new day, and temptation would take over. Sometimes in life, you just have to humble yourself, as hard as it may be, and tell someone you need help. That's not easy to do, because you fear of what people will think. I kept getting encouraged to go to Fresh Start to help me get clean and repent of my sinful lifestyle I was living in for so long. I kept dragging my feet until one day, God made it very clear to me, "Go. Go."

I called Bill Yoder who had been walking along my side, giving me council and encouragement. I said, "Bill, I'd be ready to go."

Bill did not hesitate for a minute. He said, "Let me make a phone call." A few minutes later, Bill called back and said we were flying to Indiana to Fresh Start on Monday of next week, and that's what we did.

After being in the program for almost two years at Fresh Start, when we left, we had very little to start out on, but God has been faithful and has blessed us beyond what I could have imagined. Now, I don't know if you can see the pattern as to how God never gave up on us. He is there waiting and willing to bless your life if you are there to give your heart to Him.

Buses were something I longed to have since I was a little Amish boy working in my dad's woodworking shop. God knew my heart and my desires way back when I was still a young lad at home. I always thought I would like to drive a big bus, but I never thought I would actually do it one day. He knew someday, I would give my heart to Him and serve Him with all of my heart. Of course, I failed many times along the way, no doubt, we all do, but those in Christ, when we fall, we get back up and we go again. We don't stay down.

I feel blessed far beyond imagination.

We bought this little three acres of land in Montgomery, Indiana, and we started parking the buses there, along with my woodworking shop. Mostly just a hobby shop when I'm not out on a bus run. I kept telling Malinda and my children that one day, I want to build us a house on this property. I kept that goal up, and I worked hard, doing lots of bus runs, buying more buses as the demand kept calling for more buses. We hired more drivers, which has always been our biggest challenge, to have enough drivers for all our runs we'd scheduled. Then I'd talk about one day building our house again. Finally, Amber, our youngest daughter still living at home here, kept telling me, "Dad, it'll *never* happen. You keep saying that, but it'll never happen."

Finally, my wife started saying the same thing. I started wondering if I should stop making mention of my dreams and goals of building a house, because it came to a point that every time I made mention of it, they didn't believe me anymore. I didn't know you could not keep talking about dreams and goals when you are sincere about it. I was sincere. I was excited. It was in my heart. I kept talking about it from time to time. I knew God would provide one day because his promises are true every day, if we are faithful to Him. Every time I made mention of building a house, she'd remind me that it'll never happen. Finally, I got a little stern with her to never say never. That's not how you look at life. What if the good Lord heard your comment and He held you accountable to your own words, *it'll never happen*? You got to start somewhere, and for me, it was to talk about it and pray about it. As time went on, I kept getting more and more of an urge to get this house started. About the time I thought our checking account had enough in it to maybe do something about it, either we had another major breakdown with a bus and we had to take another step back. It seemed like the business was continuously taking two steps forward and one step back. But at least, we were making progress. I felt the Lord's blessing being poured upon us. With patience, we would get there. And lots and lots of patience. So one day, I made that phone call that we were waiting on for what seemed like a long time coming, which Amber and Malinda thought would never come. I called Joe Jr. Construction to come out and take a look at the little knoll up on the west side of the shop I had there, to see what they thought about building a full in-ground basement house with the perfect full walk-out on the north side where the hill was located, an ideal spot to do this. So I thought anyway, but I guess Joe Jr. and his son didn't think so. They walked over that little knoll, surveying the idea we gave them of our future dream house.

"How about we push the front side of this knoll away and build you a house into the front of this hill and you could have the whole *front* end of the house as your walk-out?" they suggested. The back side of the house would be underground, but the whole front end would be out in the open. Joe's son, Les, seemed to think the hill was just not tall enough to build an in-ground basement and have enough fall for bathrooms in the basement like we wanted. This was a total discouragement for us. Total discouragement. Blew our dreams straight out of that little hill. Are they telling us it's not possible to build our dream home in this little hill?

Malinda and I stepped aside and talked about it for a little bit. She told me if I can't have my dream home like I want it, what is the use of building a house on this property? Did we just waste our money when we bought this property? I wondered. I told her, "Why don't we tell them we need a little more time to think over their idea?"

So they left. Our hearts sunk. We were both feeling sad. We did some more talking and walking around on that little knoll in the next few days. Several days later, I texted Les back and told him doing it the way they wanted to do it would totally blow our dream house away. I texted him to let him know we wanted to go on with our original plans, keeping the hill as is and dig a full in-ground basement with a walk-out on the north side. That if they can't do that, then it's no use we build a house there because it would not be what we had dreamed of. If we were going to build a house and put thousands of dollars in it with our hard-earned money, it better be something we would enjoy and appreciate, right? He didn't respond back until a few days later. When he did text me back, it was simply to tell us they were so busy that they probably couldn't get started on it for at least another year. We had just spoken to them earlier on that we were ready to get on with the project while we could financially do it. But I got the hint. They really didn't want to build the house the way we had asked them to. They wanted to build the house the way they thought best, not how we wanted it. And then we would probably always be using the phrase "if only." If only we could have done it the other way. So we put everything back on hold for a while again. We weren't sure if it was worth asking another builder about our dream plans for the house in the hill there or not or if they'd all be telling us the same thing. Can't be done. And about that time, the stupid COVID hit America. Never heard of such a discouraging thing as COVID, and I'm sure you all know what I'm talking about here. At the same time, Old Man Biden was running against Trump for president, and with the way COVID was going and Biden's idea was wanting to shut things back down again, we did not feel good about starting in on a new house and going in debt. If perchance Old Man Biden became president, we may never feel good about going in debt. So we held off the building project through the election time yet. Well, we all know what happened, Old Man Biden took over as president and I did not feel good about building a house if he might make a disaster out of the United States of America. What if we were halfway through building and things got shut down completely. And about that time, lumber and housing material started to skyrocket. But as I kept watching, housing construction kept right on going like there was some kind of fire behind these builders right in the midst of the battle to become president of the United States. The higher the prices went on building material, the more things seemed to boom in the building industry. So by midwinter, before Biden took over as president, lumber was three times the price what it had been before COVID. I decided if everybody else still obviously feels good about building a house, I guess it must be a sign that things are still going to be all right. Mortgage was low, and this kept housing booming even though material was outrageous high by now. COVID had taken a toll on everything. I decided since others kept going, I suppose we should too. So I talked to Marvin Graber about building our house. He came over and looked it over, and it wasn't long he had things rolling. Our dream house was going to be built, and on top of that, it was going to be built just the way we wanted it. But there was one problem. Had we started back in the fall before COVID had hit, like we originally had planned on, Marvin Graber could have framed our house, but now they were leaving on a term of working for Choice Books in Sarasota, Florida, and they would be leaving before the framing could even get started. Before Marvin and his family moved to Sarasota, he got the basement walls poured and got the ball rolling with another framer, Ferman Miller, to go up with construction. Yes, our dream house was being built. Never say never. Trust in the Lord, and He will bless you and you will prosper. We got the nicest house we have ever had in our lifetime. The house is not all that big in itself, but we put cathedral ceiling in the entire kitchen area and in the living room area, which just really opened up the space altogether. Brand-new kitchen cabinets for the kitchen which gives Malinda more cabinet space than she had ever had before. It's lovely. It's a blessing.

Something that happened on our property here, before we got started on the house though, was something I never thought I'd be praying for. Dirt. Yup, dirt. Well, that's in the next chapter of my story.

Chapter 15

God Gave Me Dirt

The "dirt story" I want to tell you about what happened about a year ago, maybe a year and a half ago already from the time I'm writing this particular chapter.

Here in our little city of Montgomery, Indiana, our Rural County Water decided to put up a new water tower in someone's field about four miles up the road from our property here, and they ran a brand-new waterline throughout the community, which meant they had to dig right through our property as well. Well, quite frankly, I believe our property got the brunt end of it. They came up the road from the east and were digging on the south side of the road all the way up until directly across the road from our property. Of all reasons unknown to me, they decided right by our property, they needed to bring that waterline underneath the road and start running it along the north side of the road up along Highway

50. Now this is the same Highway 50 that runs from the East Coast all the way to the West Coast of the United States. Runs from Washington, DC, to the state of California. And we are fortunate enough to live along this long stretch of highway. I keep saying one of these times I would like to go all the way out to Washington, DC, and start out on Highway 50, and travel it the whole way to California. Stop whenever we see something interesting enough to stop. Travel at a comfortable leisure until we made it all the way from one end to the other. Wouldn't that be an adventure in itself? Maybe when I get older and am retired, huh? Although I don't plan to ever retire. But I might take more leisure time than I can right now. Now, my real dream would be to do this with a three-wheel Honda Gold Wing motorcycle, pulling a little luggage trailer behind with us. I suppose I could write another book in itself for that trip. Maybe that will be my next book, who knows.

But anyway, let's get back to the subject of this dirt.

Real dirt.

The new water tower was out east from us on old Highway 50. This old Highway 50 joins the new Highway 50 right there by our property, coming into the shape of a Y right there.

One day as I was there at my shop working on my buses, they pulled in with this big old semi loaded down with this massive track hoe on it. Now remember, this was before we lived on this property. Our house was not yet built. Only my shop and buses were here at this time. But anyway, as they unloaded it, they then backed this track hoe right off the trailer and into the yard and then did this ninety-degree turn right there on our beautiful grass in our front yard on those massive steel tracks. It just tore that spot in our yard to pieces, not to mention with all the recent rains that we were having. They then backed this track hoe up to the area they wanted to dig at from under the road and bring this pipeline under through the road. But to do this, they first dug a huge hole right there in our front yard and put in some massive concrete barrier or something to hold back the dirt from caving in where they'd dug out. That very next day, before they could even get this concrete box put in this big hole they had dug, it rained and rained and rained some more. That massive hole filled completely up with water from all the rain, and it was running over by thousands of gallons of rainwater. All that loose dirt that was tore up when they unloaded that track hoe the day before had all been washed down to the creek in the woods as well. It was gone. This left a hole the size of New Jersey in our front yard. Okay, maybe that's stretched just a little bit, but it was like the size of a small sinkhole shaped in the form of a big bowl in the ground. It really messed up our front lawn along the road. Even more messed up when trying to mow the lawn, and I was the one doing that. Not only that, all the dirt along our property up from where they had dug that massive hole to put in this concrete barrier, that loose dirt had all been washed down the creek as well. All our good old topsoil had been washed down to the creek behind our property. I later talked to the guys working out there, and they informed me once they had completed the job, that they would come back in and fix everybody's yard back just like it had been. This sounded fair to me, and I left it at that. But the summer wore on, and slowly, they started working on some yards along the way. The grass was coming up where everything had been torn up. I couldn't mow over it because of how rough it was. Eventually, after I'd been almost ready to go see what I could do with that mess myself, they finally showed up to work on the yard and reseed it. Our yard had to be the last one they were working on. But lo and behold, they never did fill in that huge hole where they had unloaded that massive track hoe. I had been mowing through that hole all summer long after the grass came back, and it was a rough ride. I was not happy. I didn't want to jump on their case again about fixing my yard back like it was. They knew well enough what a mess they'd left for me. So one day, I called this dump truck company, one I had used previously to haul in gravel for our lot where all the buses were parked. I asked them if they had any dirt they could haul in for me. I wasn't sure just how much dirt I would need. I suspected possibly one nice big-sized load. Well, no, they didn't have any. Would you know where I might find some? They didn't know that either. Nobody had any dirt they wanted to get rid of. I wasn't so sure if they were maybe not even interested in this job or what. I told him to give me a call if they'd ever come across some dirt.

"Okay, I got your number, if I hear anything, I'll get back with you," he told me, and we hung up. I gave him two months or better, and I never did hear back from him. I knew I'd have to pay to have it hauled in, but surely, it couldn't be worse than the gravel I'd had hauled in at different times already. But none came my way. So here recently, I got an idea. I decided I would need to get a sheet of plywood, paint on it "Fill Dirt Wanted," and paint an arrow where I wanted it dumped, in case I would not be around there when it came. I wasn't sure what I might get if I asked for fill dirt. I wanted something that grass would grow in, and I could mow over it without bouncing back out of my mower seat. I had meant to get that sign made a couple weeks prior already, but suddenly, as I pulled out of my driveway one day, a gentleman flagged me down right there on the highway. He was getting ready to pull in my driveway, as I was pulling out of my driveway. He almost missed me. I pulled over; being he was in a golf cart, I knew he had to be a local. I didn't recognize him though. Guess I had never met him before.

"Could you use some dirt?" he asked.

He caught me completely off guard. How did he know I needed dirt? The yard was all green by now, but of course still very bumpy. I'd been mowing over it all summer now.

"Well, yes, I could use some," I told him. "In fact, I meant to have a sign out by the road already by this time, but I just never got to it yet."

"Well," he said, "I live right there on top of the hill. I'm your neighbor, but I guess we never met yet. I got some guys digging out my driveway, and I got several loads of dirt if you can use it."

"Absolutely. Bring it on."

I showed him where to dump it if I was not there. I came back from my run, and they had not started yet, which suited me just fine. I was hoping to be around if they came in with the dirt. Once they started, they didn't stop until they had ten loads of dirt hauled in on our property. All of a sudden, here I was scrambling for a spot to put it all. I was not about to turn away any dirt now. Not after I was not only getting it hauled in for free, but also with free delivery. At no charge. Everything was given to me. The neighbor just wanted a place to go with his dirt. I just wanted a little dirt to fill in where the contractors for the County Water had ruined my land. We dumped a total of three loads in that spot where the track hoe had torn up. I used my little twenty-five-horsepower Ford tractor and leveled it down before they'd bring in the next load. Three loads leveled that spot out perfectly like I wanted it. That's how big that hole had become. I went home that evening, telling my dear wife how blessed I was this day. I said, here I was needing this dirt for the longest time already and I was even willing to pay to get some hauled in but could not find any. Now here God sends me not only one load, but ten. I was so thankful and praised the Lord for providing for me in this way. I wasn't sure how to thank Him enough. A week later, I get a phone call.

"Hey, this is so and so with the State Highway Department. We are cleaning the shoulders of Highway 50, and we are looking for a place to dump some dirt. Could you use some dirt?"

I about fell over. Oh my. More dirt? I don't even know why they called me or where they got my number.

Well, I told him I did need some earlier on, but that need was pretty much taken care of.

"Let me take a look behind where I park the buses," I told him. "I don't know, maybe I could use some back there. Yes," I told him, "I'll go move the buses out of the way and let you dump some there."

For the next day and a half, they hauled dirt in like I had never seen before, but I was not about to turn them down. *Let them pile it up*, I thought. *Who knows, later on, I might need it.* About four days later, as I was out on a bus run, I get this phone call and I didn't recognize the number and I didn't feel like answering a soliciting phone call, so I let it go to the answering machine. Sure enough, the caller had left a message. I listened to the message.

"Hello, this is so and so, could you use any more dirt? My son is digging out a spot where they had a volleyball net set up. Might have some sand mixed in with it, but we need a place to go with it."

Oh my, what do I tell the man? No, you know what, if God wants to bless me with dirt, I will not turn it down. I called the number back and told him to go ahead and dump it where I already had a pile. Later on, I thought, *My, my, I got a lot of dirt.* A lot more dirt then I thought I had needed. But after flattening out that pile of dirt that they dumped out behind the buses, it will come in just pretty handy, I later figured out. Already got plans for it. God knew just what I needed. I was so touched by this happening, and I was reminded of the time when Jesus was out there next to the riverbank, and time was well spent already. In other words, I take it that it was toward evening and His disciples came to Jesus and told Him to send the people away that they may go buy stuff in the villages to eat for themselves. But Jesus said, "They don't need to depart. Give them to eat."

But the disciples told Him that all they had was five loaves and two fishes. That was not very much food for five thousand men, not counting all the wives and children yet. So Jesus asked them to bring the five loaves and two fishes over to Him and commanded them all to sit. And Jesus took the five loaves and two fishes and looked up into heaven; He blessed and broke and gave to the disciples and to the multitude. They did all eat and were filled, and they ended up with twelve baskets full left over yet.

So the point I see in this blessing of dirt, had I not waited on the Lord to provide for me, I would have ended up paying to have the dirt hauled in, and I would have only got but a few loads. By waiting, I got far more dirt than I thought I needed and was filled to good use. And it was free. What a huge blessing.

Chapter 16

Attitude on the Bus

Several years ago, a hurricane went through Panama City, Florida, destroying almost everything in its path. Now, several years after this major storm had long passed through, many homeowners are still waiting for a new house or having someone come fix up the damage done to their house. Many home-owners have been living in their wrecked-up house for these several years now, patiently waiting for help. Many simply had no money to fix up their house or no one was available to help them. Lots of damaged houses still sit all over the place there in Panama City. So here we get this phone call from someone asking what we would charge to run a busload to Panama City, Florida, to do a work project. So I got a price together for them what it would cost to run a bus that way. After working out a few more details about this run, Malinda and I decided why don't we do this run as team drivers because of the distance, we'd need to send two drivers on this run. By the time we would get done paying two drivers for being away for a week, this would make the trip pretty expensive, knowing these people are going down there to put in their time helping rebuild homes for these storm victims. Some drivers may donate their time on something like this, but many probably won't. So Malinda and I decided to make a price where we would not charge for our time, but just for the use of the bus. Beings the buses are so expensive to run, we cannot always just donate the bus. It takes a lot to keep these things running. One breakdown can take more to fix it than the whole trip paid us in the first place. A deal was made and the day came for us to leave. Only two couples from Daviess County, Indiana, went on this trip, the rest of the crew was from the northern part of Indiana, areas like Rochester, Indiana; LaGrange, Indiana; and a few were from Berne, Indiana. We didn't have enough passengers to fill one of the bigger buses, so we took the thirty-six-passenger coach. It was made just like the bigger coaches but only shorter. We were going to be gone nearly a week on this trip, and I believe we were all pretty excited. Some of the crew from the northern part of the state came down to Daviess County with a van and some with a truck pulling a trailer. From there, we all got on the bus. Now, two fifteen-passenger vans could have easily taken this load, but the idea was so everybody could all be together on this trip and not be crammed up in a fifteen-passenger van for nearly an eleven-hour drive. The crew was from various places,

and this would make for a much more fun, interesting trip when everybody could be in one vehicle.
Over half the crew were youth, boys and girls from
various families. So this made for one interesting
trip. Someone made mention later that we weren't
a half hour on the road when he could already tell
this was going to be one interesting trip. Sometimes,
it takes a while for everybody to kind of loosen up
and get comfortable with strangers, you know, but
it didn't take long until everybody got to know each
other pretty good on this load. This was my first time
going on such a trip, and it was a lot of fun. We all
stayed at the base of this organization, Mennonite
Disaster Service (MDS), run by the Amish out of
Lancaster, Pennsylvania. A well-organized setup and
very professional. Two single Amish men were running the show and giving us orders while we were
there. On the second day that we were there, three
Amish Pennsylvania girls showed up to put in two
weeks at the base, fixing meals. That was going to
be their job. Their names were Hanna, Rachel, and
I don't remember what the other's name was anymore. They blended right in with our crew, and we
all became best of friends quickly.

Every week, MDS gets a different crew coming
in. Malinda and I kind of had an easy job, taking the
crew to and from their places of work every morning
and bringing them back home every evening, along
with running to and fro all day long, running errands
for the crews. Every evening after supper, before anyone was to leave the supper table, each crew leader

gave a report of how their day went and what took place there. This always turned out to be the high-light of the day because once the crew leader was finished talking, it was opened up to the rest of the crew to tell something if they wished to. And that was when things got interesting. Everyone liked to pick on the others, and some very interesting things took place every day. The youth girls were out there helping right along with the men crew, and many who had no carpentry experience were now out there helping rebuilt houses. It made for lots of fun. For example, one of the girls whose name was Abby got picked on quite a bit because she liked to try to hold up her end and she would give it back to the boys if she had any opportunity to do so. But this one day, the crew she was with were hanging drywall. Not the most enjoyable job in the world. Hanging drywall is a hard job. Tiresome job. She was coming along the back, putting in screws, and was told how to put them in. Suddenly, the screw gun was making this terrible purring noise, you know like spinning the bit on a screw. And she'd spin and spin and spin that thing. That screw was not going in. She'd try another screw and the same thing. *Purr, purr.* No headways. The leader of the crew calmly went over to see what might be the problem. He took the screw gun from her, calmly switched the forward switch in the posi-tion it needed to be in, in order to drive the screw in, and drove in a couple screws. They all went in just fine and dandy. He turned the switch back to reverse position again and handed the gun back to her and told her to put a little more determination in her efforts, and he went back to what he was doing, trying to keep a straight face. *Purr, purr,* and she had *this look* on her face that this screw was going in this time. And that screw did go in, completely by spinning backward, and the look on that determined face made it go. Yup, she spun that screw in completely reversed, and she had no idea what she had just done. And unless you were with the group at suppertime when the laughter roared out after telling this story and later on at a reunion when this group came together to reminisce and the three Pennsylvania girls showed up as well.

And that gives a little insight of that trip. But the real thing that got me to write this part of the story was this. The attitude. What a difference an attitude can make. It can make or break a situation. The point I want to make here was the bus ride. For starters, unless you were ever with a group to go on a work project like this one or just simply on a sightseeing tour, you will surely have to agree there was not much that will beat the fun with having everybody together like this. When you are traveling in two or three vans following each other, you never know what fun you are missing out in the van behind you. You can't hear their conversations. With the bus, everyone was together. Now I suppose there are some out there that might disagree with me on this, but unless you have ever done it this way, you really don't know the difference. On our way down to Panama City, our bus ride went just as smooth as hunky-dory.

It went lovely. One afternoon, the crew came in early from work, and we all got in the bus and rode about an hour south to see the water. The ocean. Some on the bus had never seen the ocean. It was a lovely treat after several days of hard work. And it was a highlight of the trip as well. On our way home, things didn't go quite so hunky-dory. Malinda was driving, and it was a few minutes after midnight, I was sleeping up in the front seat. We took turns to drive, being it was nighttime driving. Suddenly, as we were approaching Nashville, Tennessee, four hours from home, a red flashing light came on the dash of the bus. Malinda reached over and woke me up, asking what this little red flashing light was all about. It was midnight. Everything was quiet inside the bus at this time of the night. Everyone was sleeping or trying to be sleeping, I don't know which. Probably some of both. I got up and looked the gauge over real good. Everything looked good as far as I could tell. The temperature gauge looked all right; the symbol on the flashing light looked like it might possible be showing a tire that was low. So I told Malinda to just keep going. We'd check the tires when we would switch drivers next. I was tired. All I wanted was to go back to sleep. The others were all sleeping, and I didn't want to pull over and disturb everyone. I wasn't back in my seat very long when this obnoxious beep blurted out of the dash along with now the second red flashing light. I quickly got up and looked the gauges all over again. Couldn't see anything alarming. This was strange. This was our latest bus we had just purchased, and

I was not yet familiar with all the flashing lights and all the whistles of this bus just yet. But I was about to learn and not in a good way either. Yikes. All our other buses we owned were MCI models. This one was a Van Hool, which looks completely different on the dash than our other buses. So I was not familiar with this blaring buzzer going off or the two flashing lights. The beeping noise came from underneath the steering wheel somewhere, below the dash. While Malinda was still driving, going seventy miles an hour, I got a flashlight and lay down on my back, on the floor, and reached in under the steering wheel area there and found this little square box where the loud beeping sound was coming from. Good thing it was otherwise dark inside of the bus. But I found two wires going to the box, and it was easy enough to undo the wires. So I pulled the one wire away from that little red boxy thing, and the obnoxious noise shut off. Whew, now I can finally go back to sleep. I got back in my seat like I knew what I was doing, and I wanted to go back to sleep before it was my turn to drive again. Malinda kept right on driving. We got through Nashville and were probably a half hour north of Nashville when suddenly, Malinda says the bus was losing power. She pulled off the side of the road, and just like that, the motor died. It was dead. Deader than a door knob. I got out of the bus to go to the back end and see if it might be out of coolant. When I opened the door and looked back there, my heart sunk. The smoke was just rolling in whirls back there, and I could see that this motor was boiling hot.

Yup, no water. And we had no water or coolant on the bus either. It was pitch-black dark outside on this October night as we were traveling home from having a wonderful time of working together. But now this. Not good at all. Did we just ruin this little coach by not taking heed of those red flashing lights on the dash? That little red flashing light really did mean something.

We were now sitting beside the road on a long upgrade hill along I-24, northwest of Nashville, Tennessee. I tried to call twenty-four-hour road service but couldn't seem to get anybody interested to come help us at this time of the morning. We were still three hours from home. It was just past midnight. What to do? So I called Tim Weaver, one of my drivers. Luckily, he answered. I had him bring one of the other buses to rescue us that I knew had several gallons of antifreeze on board underneath in storage. There we sat; everybody pretty much curled up on a seat, sleeping till the other bus showed up. When Tim showed up, we put antifreeze in that tank. Cranked that motor and it fired right up, but oh, it did not look or sound good. My stomach did a flip. In fact, I think my stomach felt about as bad as that motor did by now. I knew there was something terrible wrong with that bus. The white smoke just poured out of that exhaust pipe. Did I just blow up that little motor? We had bought that little coach about eight months earlier, and it was the finest, smoothest little riding coach. We had already put lots of miles on it without any issues. It just ran and ran and ran. Well, until now.

To make a long story short without boring you more on those little details, yes, we had to get in the other bus and the little one needed to be towed. And the worst part of it was the motor was a goner. It had gotten so hot that it had melted parts of the motor on the inside. It needed a new motor. Hard expensive lesson was learned. Listen to those little warning signs when they come up on the dash. First off, that first little light that had come on was a warning light to let the driver know it was low in coolant and needed some added. All would have been well. The second light that came on, along with the blaring beep, was a dire warning, "Pull over, your motor is hot." We didn't heed it either. Yikes.

We have since put in a new motor, and that thing has again done well for us. We learned the hard way that time.

Being the owner of the bus company on top of yet being one of the drivers is something I'm not sure I can honestly tell you what it feels like being broken down beside the road with a load of people on the bus. I never know if the load is going to be upset with me or if they will be understanding. I've had both.

You know, as hard as I try to stay on top of the buses mechanically and keep them in good running order, there are always times when you just can't get everything right. These machines are made by humans. They have a tendency to have parts wear out or go bad occasionally. There are many, *many* moving parts on a bus. The thing is, some people still think that a bus should never break down while you are out on the road. And if I had my way, that would be true, believe me. I've learned that the buses seldom break down while they are sitting in the driveway.

But the load we had with us this time were understanding. Sometimes, things go wrong. Up until this happened, we were having a really good trip. Lots of fun, hard work, and getting to know people we had never met before. We were like family on that bus within one week's time.

So then, just several months later, getting into our regular weekly Florida runs to Sarasota, I had two other drivers on a bus headed to Florida. Most of the time, I was one of the drivers when we head for Sarasota, but I wasn't this time. This time, the drivers were Joe Miller and I forget who the other driver was that went with him. I didn't find out about this until a little later than, but this one driver who was on this bus at that time told me something over the phone that I had not heard before. We were talking bus talk, and he told me he needed to tell me something. I was like "Oh no, now what."

"Well," he said, "I want to pass on a compliment on to you. On our run to Florida, we had this one passenger that came up, and we had this lengthy talk during the night while I was driving This fella was telling me about the good trip that he was privileged to be with on this Panama City, Florida, trip several weeks earlier on one of your buses and how that was one of his best trips he had taken in a long time. After a little while I got to thinking, now wait a minute, was this not the trip that Nealie was on and the bus broke down? So I asked this fella again. Going back to our earlier conversation about that Panama City, Florida, trip, was that not the trip the bus broke down on the way home and you had to sit there until another bus came to pick you all up? 'Oh, yes, that was the one,' he said. 'Well, you just said it was one of your best trips. The bus breaking down was probably kind of a letdown, wasn't it?' 'Oh yeah, I had actually already forgot about the breakdown,' he chuckled. 'You know, we had some really good drivers on the bus and everything was going so good until that happened, but I guess we overlooked that incident. The rest of the trip made up for it,' he said."

So Joe tells me, "Nealie, saying all this, that bus breaking down like it did, should have or definitely could have ruined that whole trip for everybody."

And he was right, it could have.

"But I just wanted to pass that good compliment on to you as it was told to me," Joe told me.

I always like to hear good reports, but unfortunately, they are not always good. Some people get grumpy when their plans have to get changed because of a breakdown or something doesn't go as planned. To be quite honest, I think I probably feel worse than anyone on the bus, when it comes to any kind of bus trouble. But God is still good. We are a blessed people.

So here is my thing on this whole thing. When I am on the bus as a driver, I do my best to make the trip comfortable and fun for all the passengers. I can't always please everybody, but I sure will do my best to. I try to take the curves, on-ramps, off-ramps slow and easy to make where the passengers do not wake up during the night from my reckless driving. Same way during the day. Easy, slow takeoffs. You do not need to punch that pedal to the floor. That will not impress nobody, especially not me. You just blew a half gallon of fuel out that exhaust pipe and didn't gain nothing but show off your reckless driving and cost me a half gallon of fuel. Slowdowns need to be nice and easy smooth and slow to a complete stop. That's what passengers like. A nice, easy, smooth, and safe bus ride. Malinda and I could have made this Panama City bus ride uneasy and not a real fun experience, depending on our attitude. In fact, let me give you a quick little story about one of my former bus drivers I had to let go because of his attitude toward my passengers. This one trip I had I'll call him Jim and Ronnie on this run to Pennsylvania. On the way home from that trip, Jim goes on the intercom and makes this announcement that the front half of the bus must please put their shoes back on. It was unbearable stinky up front here.

He was referring to the stinky feet he was smelling. Well, I would never had found out about this if the passengers hadn't made the remark that they do not want Jim for a driver again. They want Ronnie to be their driver the next time. And that was not the only thing he said to turn off the passengers.

Your attitude can go a long way, and that's a fact. And that is my point here.

We found out through this one passenger who was talking with Joe that night on the way to Sarasota, Florida, that the breakdown did not affect his idea of having a good trip.

"Nealie," Joe told me, "that's a compliment worth sharing. You guys did such a great job of driving that they overlooked that breakdown. Seriously."

So I want to pass this along to anyone who is reading this, your attitude can make a huge difference as to how people respond to you. It can make or it can break. You can make it fun and enjoyable or you can make it miserable for everybody. The trip was so enjoyable for everybody that we even had a reunion get-together four months later in Macy, Indiana, at one of our passengers' homes. Almost everybody showed up, and we again shared the highlights of the trip. Those are trips I thoroughly enjoy. That trip right there ended up costing me just under thirty thousand dollars, after a new motor, tow-truck cost, and everything else that went with it. But we have to keep putting one foot in front of the other and keep going.

Chapter 17

The Homeless Man Who Wanted to Get on the Bus

This week, Malinda and I were team driving the Florida bus, and as we were loading up right there in Pinecraft at the Tourist Mennonite Church parking lot, like we always do every week, we do a "list call," making sure we got all the passengers on the bus that had tickets to head northbound. After we did this, it was confirmed that we were loaded. We had everyone counted for, and we had one empty seat left on the bus. So this one Amish fella jokingly made this remark about maybe we can find a homeless guy along the way to fill that seat. And it just so happened that this widow lady was the one sitting by herself next to this empty seat. She piped right up, "No, I'm not having no homeless guy sit beside me."

Otherwise, the bus was fully loaded in the top as well as down below in the bays. For some reason, it seemed like we are always more packed full down below in the bays going northbound than we are heading southbound, most of the time. Somehow, people accumulate things while they are vacationing in Florida to take back home. After we did the list call and were sure we had everyone on the bus, we headed out to Interstate 75, and we were on our way. Along the way, we always stopped about every three hours for a short restroom break and enough time to grab a cup of fresh coffee if you like. Our first stop on the way home was always our regular supper stop at this Pilot truck stop with a Wendy's. We always tell everyone to order their food to go so that we can keep moving right on home. I know eating on the bus makes for a lot more clean-up time back home, but it's a sacrifice we are willing to take so that we can keep right on moving toward home. After about fifteen minutes back on the road, the second driver then gets a trash bag and starts from the rear of the coach, working the way toward the front, gathering all the supper trash. This really helps to not have this trash lying all over the floor while traveling.

Now, I need to tell you something, at this time, I did not know about this remark that had been made about picking up a homeless guy along the way home to fill this empty seat. I was still unaware of that remark that had been made. But as we got to our supper stop there, Malinda got off the bus first like she always does and headed right in to order our food right away so that we, as drivers, could eat before we head back out. In fact, I always try to call ahead to the restaurant about thirty minutes before we would arrive to give them a little heads-up that we are coming and how many passengers we got. Most of the time, this really speeds up the process for us. The restaurant is ready and waiting on us by the time we arrive. Malinda is usually the first one back out to the bus with the food being she was the first off the bus. After I'd gotten my coffee, I get back out to the bus and quickly eat my sandwich if I can before we head out. Sometimes, I will sit in my seat to eat; other times, I will stand on the outside to stretch my legs while I have the chance to do so. On this particular evening, I decided to stand on the outside of the bus to eat my sandwich. While I was standing outside, eating my sandwich, there he came. The homeless fella. He came from the back of the bus. Came walking straight toward me. I didn't think anything about it except I expected for him to very likely beg for some money. I immediately saw that he was a homeless man, dirty, shaggy-looking clothes and bags hanging over his shoulders that he was carrying with him. He walked right up to my face, and he looked me straight in the eyes with pleading eyes, begging eyes, asking for a ride to Atlanta, Georgia. I was like, "Oh, help."

I knew we would be going right through Atlanta, Georgia. Right where he wanted to go. How do I tell him we cannot take him? Our time of going through Atlanta, Georgia, was always around midnight. That's a fun time to drive through Atlanta. I always enjoy driving through Atlanta at that time of the night. Most of the time, we can sail right on through with traffic not being heavy at all. All the different shapes and types of tall buildings and the lights that decorate the city of these buildings was remarkable as one drove dead smack through the center of town like this. Most of our drivers, I believe, all enjoy driving through Atlanta in the middle of the night like this. But when Malinda and I team drive, I don't get the chance to drive through Atlanta because of how our driving switches are scheduled, taking turns to drive. She does not like to drive over Monteagle, Tennessee, which is a 5 percent grade mountain, four miles up and four miles back down. So I always drive the shift that will get us over that mountain. This puts her in the shift to drive through Atlanta. I believe she enjoys the drive through that big city as much as anyone of us drivers do.

So getting back to this homeless fella. How would I go about to avoid telling him that we are actually going right through Atlanta? For the sake of our passengers, I told him I could not do that. I don't have room on the bus for him.

"We are loaded," I told him.

"Please, man. Let me ride to Atlanta. Please, please."

Again, I told him I cannot do that.

"Please, please. I got a ticket right here," he said as he pulled out a white piece of paper.

"Oh, you're looking for the Greyhound bus," I told him. "They load right there across the street over there," I told him, pointing across the road.

Often, when we pull in this Pilot truck stop, there will be one, two, and sometimes three Greyhound buses sitting over across the street there while we are over here on the other side of the road. So I was hoping he got us mixed up with the Greyhound bus. But he didn't flinch for a second, but looked me straight in my eyes again. "Please, please."

Again, I told him I could not do that, that we had a full bus. At this time, I did not yet know about the homeless remark that was made earlier nor did I know we only had the one seat open yet. Malinda had not told me this until after this episode took place.

"Please, please."

I kept saying, "No. No."

"Please don't do this to me. Please, please. Please don't do this to me."

His voice was of a sincere plea, and it affected my spirit because of the tone of his voice. His plea sounded to be coming from a true genuine heart.

"Please, please give me a ride to Atlanta. Please, please. I will give you ten dollars," he told me. "That is all I have."

I told him ten dollars would not get him to Atlanta. He tried to show me his ticket, but I didn't look at it close enough to see if it was actually a Greyhound bus ticket or what he had. I'm assuming it was though. But the tone of his voice and the plea was so sincere that it almost hurt to not help the man. But I just kept telling him I couldn't do it. I had my responsibilities with my people on the bus, and I needed to keep them safe and comfortable. I needed to take care of my load. After much pleading, he finally gave up and walked away. He went right straight over to a pickup truck that had the hood propped up next to a gas pump, wrenches lying on the radiator and a couple antifreeze jugs or maybe they were transmission fluid jugs, I don't know. But I see he was talking to this fella for only a few minutes. The homeless guy should have known a truck with his hood propped up and tools lying all over the engine was probably not the wisest choice if he wanted to get to Atlanta, Georgia, but I guess he was desperate. From there, he went over to the next vehicle and the last I saw of him was walking away from that truck as well. I never did see him after that.

Afterward, a few of us got to talking about this situation, and we suspected that he could very likely been kicked off the Greyhound bus across the street just a few minutes earlier, and he saw our bus over across the street here, and he quickly decided to try getting a ride with us. I don't know that for sure of course, but it could been very possible.

I struggled for a while whether I did the right thing or if I should have let the guy on the bus and given him a ride to Atlanta since we were going right through there anyway. What if once we had him on the bus, we could not get him back off? What if? These are times one just never knows what was the right or wrong thing to do. I felt sorry for the guy, especially after hearing the tone of his voice that sounded so real. Like a child pleading.

A few days later, as I thought about this whole situation, I got another picture that will one day be very real for many people. I was standing at the door of my bus. It was loaded with passengers who had bought their tickets ahead of the departure date. They were on the bus and felt safe. This stranger who walked up to me was pleading to get in the bus. I was standing my ground.

"Please, please," he begged, but I kept on telling him I could not let him in.

"Please, please don't do this to me," he begged.

One day, many people will be pleading to get in while Jesus stands at the door. According to Matthew 7:21–23 Jesus will say, "Depart from me, I cannot let you in."

"Please, please. Please do not do this to me. Please do not do this to me."

But Jesus will deny them access into the pearly gates of heaven. What a sad day that will be. No pleading and no amount of begging will get you in after it's too late. We must search our hearts and be ready before that awful day so we can enter into the gates of heaven so that there will be a seat left open for us and a ticket with our name on it or, in this case, our name in the Book of Life.

Chapter 18

The Homeless Couple Who Wanted a Bed

Recently, Malinda and I made a bus run to Mechanicsville, Maryland, with a load of Amish. After we dropped them off in the community there, we were turned loose for a couple days before we would need to pick them up again. It seemed the most decent motel available was in La Plate, Maryland, about thirty minutes away. We didn't do much running around in this town, so I really don't know just how it was for homeless people as far as that. But we did have a run-in with this one homeless couple who wanted help. Now before I go there though, when I saw how close we were to Washington, DC, I got this idea to leave the bus set at the motel, and we go rent a car for the next day and we go explore Washington, DC. I've been to Washington, DC, several times already for a tour, but Malinda had never seen Washington, DC, yet. The last time I was there was when Trump was president, and I had a busload there touring the town. One of the youth girls on the bus had googled info of the White House, and she found out that Trump was flying out of the White House that afternoon. So about that time we all walked over as close to the White House as we were allowed to and thought we'd watch, possibly, we might see Trump fly out. Suddenly, here they come, three extremely low-flying Air Force One helicopters. It was like they suddenly came out of nowhere. Two of them flew on by, but one went down and landed right in the front lawn of the White House. We were in a real good place to watch. I had my binoculars with me, and I was all eyes. This was a real highlight of the trip for me. Of course, Air Force One was blocking the view from the door which Trump was going to walk from to this helicopter. We watched as this massive big Air Force One helicopter lifted off the lawn of the White House and turned and came flying straight overhead of us flying very, *very* low, now again joined with the other two who came from out of nowhere. These guys got their act together, and they know what they are doing as far as security goes to protect the president. It was a sight to behold for sure.

But now here we were, Malinda and I. I wanted to take this opportunity to show her around Washington, DC, since we were only thirty minutes away. We did a lot of walking. Parking is a big problem around there, so we parked in one area, and we did a lot of walking. Lo and behold, while Malinda and I were not far away from the White House, this time around again, here come the three Air Force One copters, this time flying Mr. Biden out. I was not nearly as thrilled to watch Biden fly out as I was the time President Trump flew out. Wonder why, hmmm. In fact, I never even took a picture of the action of Biden's departure. But I still have Trump on camera and video both.

We had a wonderful day touring Washington, DC, and Arlington Cemetery and the change of the guards. It was a worthwhile day for sure for Malinda and me.

Back to the town of La Plate. Malinda and I decided to walk down to Starbucks for the evening to get us a coffee drink, maybe relax a little while we were in the lobby drinking our coffee. As Malinda and I started down the sidewalk, we saw this couple trying to cross the street from the other side of the highway on this very busy highway. Obviously, the walkway by the crossroads a hundred feet up by the red light must not have been suitable for them to cross. They wanted to cross where it was actually illegal to cross. Right where the traffic was still moving heavily. It was very obvious the couple was having a bad day. They were loudly yelling and talking in a rough tone of voice to each other. They were arguing while crossing a busy highway. As they came across the highway there, basically meeting up at the same location where Malinda and I were, I didn't necessarily even give it a thought that they were about to approach us for help.

Now, I'd been after Malinda for the last whole hour to go for Starbucks, but she just couldn't drop her bookwork it seemed like. She carries her bookwork and the business phone wherever we go. Yes, it was high time for us to look into getting a secretary, but so far, we've been trying to carry the whole load ourselves, doing bus runs and bookwork all at the same time.

That part made it very nice because we know exactly what's going on within the business. But it's time to let a secretary carry part of that load. We could enjoy our trips even better if she didn't need to do bookwork while we were at the motels.

But we messed around for an hour or better, probably more like two hours, before we finally made it out of our room and headed down the sidewalk toward Starbucks. During that time, I made numerous comments about going for coffee. "Let's go. Let's go." But it just wasn't the right time for Malinda to pull away from her work. Then there were more phone calls to answer. Finally, it was time to go; it was about to get dark on us out there.

The man met right up with Malinda and me as he came across the road pushing his way through heavy-moving traffic, zigzagging his way across the busy highway. It appeared he was so heavy into an argument with his wife that it appeared he was just hoping to get hit and killed by a car. That's what it appeared like to me as I watched him come across the highway. The lady was doing the same, zigzagging across the highway, trying to dodge traffic, but she came to the sidewalk a little farther down the road. With the heavy traffic, she didn't make it straight across to where we were. It appeared she was sort of ignoring his screams, yet she would yell back at him. I still had the slightest clue that he might approach us as I was witnessing this.

"Sir, look, could you guys please help my wife and me? We have no place to go. Nothing."

He was wearing a black mask on his face, the COVID-19 mask, and she was also wearing a mask. The mask that he was wearing was dirty and looked as you can imagine a homeless person's clothing. Dirty and plenty of wear.

"We were just denied a room from that motel right over yonder," and he pointed to the motel across the road from the direction he came from. He flashed the credit card they had tried to use, and there was no more credit left on it. Not until they put more money on the card tomorrow. And he told us certainly tomorrow there would be more money put on the card, and they would be good to go again until the rest of their money came in. They just needed a room for tonight. He was begging for us to buy them a room. He was a nonstop-talking fella and so I cannot even remember everything we talked about in that short of time we had met him. A few minutes into trying to persuade us to help them out, he yelled at her by name to come over and join us.

"Be respectful," he yelled at her.

237

Before she made her way over to join us, Malinda said, "Sir, it appeared like you guys were in an argument. We heard you."

He was very quick to admit, "Yes, we were in an argument. I'm trying to convince her I will have a good bed for her tonight, but absolutely nothing is working out for us and we absolutely have *nothing. Nothing*," he stressed loudly once again. "Please. Please help us," with praying hands, he pleaded. "Please, we got nothing. No place to sleep tonight. Please do it for the sake of my wife."

I would have liked to see his actual face with the face mask off his face and the lady's, but they were covered under that mask on their faces. To this day, I can't believe I didn't ask him to uncover his face so we could see who we were talking to. On top of that, he declared they would pay us back the very next day as soon as they got more money on their card.

"How can you pay us back from a card?" I asked.

"Ooh, we can go to any ATM once we have money on the card, it is just today that we have nothing on the card," he responded. "We are screwed until tomorrow," he assured us.

After that they would be okay again, he informed me very firmly. They wanted our cell phone number so they could reach us as soon as they'd have the money available in the morning.

Hmmm, how risky is that? I wondered to myself. Well, isn't too much they can do with my cell number, so I gave him my number. We got their number as well, as they were carrying a smartphone.

After pleading with us for several minutes, I asked him if Malinda and I could have a moment to discuss this, just the two of us.

"Yes, absolutely," he obliged.

Did this mean there was hope for him? I wondered. Not sure what was going through his head at this time. I felt for the couple, but I didn't want to help out someone into something that I wasn't sure of the situation. Only God really knew. How could we know the real truth? We couldn't see the man's real heart. Only his heart's cry, but was it genuine?

Malinda and I stepped aside for a few minutes to talk privately what we should do in a situation like this. We decided we probably don't help people like this out often enough. The thing was, you just never know what they will do with the money when you hand them cash. The motel they wanted to stay in was straight back across the road, the direction where they had just come from. So we told them we would not give them any money, but we will walk with them over to the motel and buy them a room. We would see if their word was as good as they told us it was. They promised to pay us back the very next day. We walked into this motel, and we could immediately tell by the looks of the person behind the counter with a sheet of glass between me and him that he had a serious look on his face like he knew what was coming. Immediately, I got the feeling this was not the first time this couple came in with someone else to pay for their room, but I decided to follow on through. We paid for their room, and they ever so much thanked us for it. Were they genuine about paying us back? Malinda and I decided if they were true to their word and they would call us back the very next day offering to pay us back, we would then let them know we do not want the money back. It's a gift to them; we now know they truly needed a room for the night. We would thank them for wanting to pay us back, but we would, out of our kindness, give it as a gift to someone truly in need.

Now we would wait and see. Are they honest people like they told us they were? The next day came and went, and we never heard back from them. The second day came and went, and we never heard back from them. So did the rest of the days. Today, we still did not hear back from them. So in conclusion, we felt like we did our part as much as we knew to do. We also now know, not always are the homeless out there being honest when they beg for money, which of course always was a question for any of us. Will they always use the money wisely, or bed in this case, as they begged of us?

Now I still have a question, how do you know when you should truly give and when you shouldn't? When is it okay to give and when is it not? Does perhaps Matthew 25 come to play here or how do we discern? Food for thought. Everyone has a different answer, I know. But for tonight, these folks had a bed to sleep in.

Chapter 19

The Lost Pocketbook

As far as I can remember, I had an average day at work, except for the fact of another usual Wednesday evening rush. I never did like the Wednesday evening rush thing, trying to make it home from work in time, get cleaned up, and if I was lucky, get a bite to eat, rush out the door, and off to church for Wednesday evening prayer service. I enjoyed prayer service. I don't think there is a thing wrong with that. In fact, it is a good thing. I believe the Lord is honored to have people come together and pray, but to make someone feel guilty for not being able to make it to prayer time, I don't believe this should be done. I believe prayer can be done while you are on the road, at work, in the shower, in bed, or wherever you are at. I enjoy meeting with the church folks to pray, when I can.

On this particular evening though, it wasn't our normal Wednesday evening church service, it was going to be our normal monthly men's meeting. I had to rush around in order to get to church on time, and I was a few minutes late according to the clock, but unfortunately, others were also running a bit late this evening, and the meeting had not started yet. I didn't feel so out of place now.

It was a real cold winter day, and the old house we lived in was hard to keep warm. Before I left for the meeting that evening, I told my wife I've had enough of this uncomfortable cold house we were renting at the time, having to wear a sweater of something to stay warm. Right after men's meeting tonight, I would run on up to Walmart and buy us a couple larger space heaters.

I didn't stick around very long after the meeting like usual, eating cookies and drinking coffee and chatting with the other men. I got me a cup of coffee to go and left for Walmart. Of all things, I got to Walmart, and here sits Mark Miller's car already. Wow, I thought I was the first one to leave the meeting, but I guess not. I pulled right over next to his car. Mark was still sitting there in his car but didn't notice me pull up beside him. I got out of my little Astro van, knocked on his car window, and kept right on walking. It was getting late, and I was in a hurry. The wind was howling pretty good, and just the walk from my van to the front doors of Walmart was long enough of a walk for me through the cold wind. I had on a leather jacket, and the cold wind soaked right on through that leather jacket it seemed.

We already had a couple small space heaters in the house the way it was, but they were not able to keep that old house warm. Walmart didn't seem to have a good option of heaters, but I got two that would have to do the job. As I rushed toward the counters, pushing my cart loaded with the two big boxes of heaters, here come a couple guys walking toward me. One of them being a friend to one of my daughters, of course, he stopped to chat a bit. I think we must've talked for twenty minutes or more. Did I mention I was in a hurry? But we all need friends, right? Cannot always ignore them and move on. I know I probably do that too much. I paid for my purchase and headed for the van. I had a good twenty-five miles to get to my home. At the counter, I remember having people behind me in line waiting to pay as well. So I wanted to make it as quick as possible for the others behind me. I stuck my change in my pocketbook and slipped my pocketbook right into my leather jacket pocket, which, by the way, does not have the deepest of pockets. But I didn't think anything of it.

Out by the van, I wanted to put the heaters in the back of the van, but the two swinging doors kept trying to swing shut, banging against me by the strong cold wind howling all around me, making it wintery miserable. I kept using my elbows to push the doors back open, but they would just swing back and hit me harder in the side. This was getting really annoying. I don't suppose it would have been so bad if it hadn't been for the cold wind. I guess I just really

243

despise the cold. I prefer warm weather over cold. Mark Miller's car still sat there when I left.

When I got home, the house was dark. The lights had all been turned off already, and the rest of my family had went to bed. I was glad for them, and yet at the same time, I never did like coming home like this from a meeting or shopping and then go straight to bed. I like coming home, stretch out a bit, relax before I hit the sack, you know. Unwind a bit first.

I carried the heaters to the house and planned to set them up without waking anyone. I tried to tread softly as I walked around the old crackling wood floor.

When I got inside, I put my hand in my coat pocket; lo and behold, my pocketbook was gone. The immediate feeling you get when your pocketbook is not where you know it ought to be—uhh, not a good feeling. I felt all around my jacket, but there was absolutely no pocketbook to be felt bulging anywhere in my jacket. I quickly turned and went back out the door to my little van to see if it would, by chance, have fallen out inside of the van. The side pockets in the van door, but nope. Under the seat? Nope. All over the van floor? Nope. I mean, it was nowhere to be found. Surely, I must be overlooking somewhere. I'm just all nerved up, I reminded myself. So I started back in the same routine search again. All through the van door pockets, under the seat, on the floor, outside around the van, but that pocketbook was nowhere in sight. I walked back in toward the house searching in my footsteps when I carried the heaters to the house. The security light outside was well lit and made it easy to see. But there was no trace of dropping the pocketbook along the way in. Okay, by now, I decided it was time to wake my wife and see if she could help me locate it. I have often found that she can find things even when they might lay right there in plain sight, and somehow, I could so easily overlook it. This could possibly be the case again. I couldn't wait until morning to continue the search. So I went in and I woke her up. This was not a good feeling, and I hated to do this. My space heaters were not set up yet, and now my pocketbook was lost and it was way past bedtime. I had to get up early the next morning to pick up the workers where I worked at Graber Steel and Fab. I needed plenty of sleep so I could make it through the next day. Welding had a tendency to make you sleepy. I hated to fight sleep at work.

I went in the bedroom and woke up my wife.

"Hey, I think I just lost my pocketbook. I cannot locate it."

"Where'd you put it?" she asked.

"Right here in my leather jacket pocket," I told her.

I remembered so well of putting it right in there in my pocket because I had a line of people behind me. I remembered when I stuck it in my pocket that it didn't go in very deep. Because the pockets were just not very deep. I think I had planned once I got out to the van, away from the people behind me in line, that I would put the pocketbook in another pocket that would seem more comfortable and safe. But once I had left the counter, I forgot all about relocating my pocketbook elsewhere. Malinda got up from her sleep, and we both went out to the van and went through the very same routine searching, but no pocketbook. I was thinking, *This is the last time I will stick my pocketbook in my leather jacket pocket again.* I had just put several hundred dollars cash in my pocketbook a week earlier. The reason I remember about the couple hundred dollars in my pocketbook was because the boys and I had gone to town, and just in case we find Christmas gifts, I wanted to be prepared. We ended up not buying anything then and I knew they were still in there. That bugged me a lot.

Then I remembered my friends I had met at Walmart. Could it be that they might still be there? So I quickly called one of them. To my surprise, they were actually still there. I had them walk out to the parking lot in the area where I had been. I had this weird feeling that my pocketbook very likely fell out when those van doors kept swinging shut on me, and I kept taking my elbow to swing them back open. I started feeling pretty dumb for putting it in my shallow pocket of my leather jacket, knowing it didn't go in very far to begin with.

When my friend called back, he reported that they could not find anything. What a bummer. I was not really surprised because I was parked right up in the front area of Walmart where it was all lit up. If it lay on the pavement anywhere there, it would surely been spotted right away. So then I quickly called Walmart service center and reported my lost pocketbook just in case someone would be honest enough to take it in to the service center if it was found. I was at a loss. Where else could I turn to now? I mean, I looked everywhere I possibly could. I retraced my steps numerous times back and forth from the house to the van. Nothing.

Prayer? Prayer, what would that do now? My, my, I should've prayed long before this. Because by now, we've looked everywhere possible, and so what would prayer help, right? I mean, I believe in miracles, because I've had many miracles in my own life already up until now. That's the purpose of sharing these events with you in hopes you will see God's mighty power and the power of prayer. I need these types of problems sometimes in my life even though they are not fun to experience at the moment, but so I fall down on my face time and time again and realize without God, I'm nothing. I can't do everything on my own. I need help. Even while going through the program at Fresh Start, I saw many miracles in my life. No doubt God could locate that thing for me, and He already knows exactly where it was. Will He show me?

Then the feeling came to me, yeah, probably the pocketbook will possibly show up at Walmart service center, but the cash would be all gone. So while I was standing right there on the outside of the van and Malinda was in the back of the van searching, I whispered a prayer to God, "Lord, you know exactly where my pocketbook is and you could show me where it is. I know that wouldn't be hard for you. Lord, if you want, please let me find it. I pray this in Jesus's name. Amen."

Immediately, I started feeling doubt that it could be found, because I waited too long to pray and we've looked everywhere already. I walked toward the house and started up the steps, right after I finished praying, retracing my steps once more. As I started up the steps—wait a minute, what's that lying beside the steps? Lo and behold right there lay my pocketbook. I was absolutely floored, *for real*. I could just not believe my eyes. I had only finished praying for a minute by the time I reached the steps, and God had already answered my prayer. Talk about a miracle. Talk about God answering prayer. This was just about more than I could grasp to be true. Why I couldn't see that thing lying there earlier was beyond my mind.

And then Satan started planting thoughts of *Yeah, right, you would've found it anyway. It's not just because you prayed.*

But you know what, I chose to believe otherwise. I will choose to believe the Lord had opened my eyes to find my pocketbook because I had asked. I choose to believe God still works miracles just as he did back in the stories we read in the Bible times. He still does today. Matthew 7:7 says, "Ask and it shall be given you, seek and you shall find."

I praise the Lord for his faithfulness and goodness to me. My pocketbook has been found.

Chapter 20

The Lost Cell Phone

Now I'm not sure if this is where this chapter actually fits in, but I wanted to share yet this one amazing story that took place sometime soon after we had graduated from Fresh Start. I wrote this chapter back right after it took place so that I wouldn't forget the details of it. So now, I'm just throwing it in here toward the back part of my book. I wanted to share it because of how it had touched me back then. My hope is that it will touch you in some way like it touched me. Stories like this is where my faith gets strengthened because of the miracles of God. The prayers that God answers when we ask. I guess God knows I need these miracles.

Friday afternoon at work there at Graber Steel, just all at once, with hardly any prior warning, I got the flu bug very quickly. My bones started aching all over and deep behind my eyes started aching. It quickly got bad enough that I had to go home. I knew the feeling that I was having was definitely the flu bug. Most commonly, that's how my flu arrived, in my bones and in behind my eyes, achy painy.

I went home and lay down for several hours and rested. Then I went back to my work area in time to take the workers home again in the evening. The following day was Saturday, which I had planned a busy day working in my little hobby shop, making wood crafts for the flea-market booth. I had enough things ready to go that it would take half a day going to the two flea markets to restock.

When Saturday morning rolled around, I absolutely did not feel up to doing the flea-market restocking. There goes another Saturday by, and I won't get anything done that I wanted to. Saturdays were pretty precious. It was the only day I get to spend working around home. But as it turned out then, my wife offered, or maybe it was more that I talked her into it, I don't remember which, but she went with me and drove while I sort of lay back in the passenger seat next to her. I didn't have the stomach flu. It was just the aching of my bones all over and my eyes.

We went in to the little city of Washington and restocked the booth there and then on down to Jasper and did the same thing there. Reuben, our youngest son, wanted to ride along, and so after we were ready to head back home, we stopped by McDonald's to get Reuben his fries. His mouth had been watering for the last full thirty minutes for some McDonald's fries.

Malinda ran in to get some food while I stayed out in the van, resting my achy bones. Before she went in, she had asked if I would do her a favor. She wanted me to call home and have Loretta and the rest of the children get showered and cleaned up for Sunday. I reached for my cell phone hanging on the right side of my belt, but lo and behold, there was no cell phone in my phone holder.

The cell phone was gone, but my pouch was still there. How in the world did this happen? I don't remember what kind of thoughts all went through my mind in that short of time, but as you can imagine, at times like this, when you lose something this precious, your mind goes a hundred and twenty miles an hour. Your head starts a-spinnin'.

I reach again, but the phone pouch was empty. But I noticed something. My pouch was hanging upside down on my belt, and the phone was gone. I had to retrace my memory back to the flea market. My phone must've surely slipped out while I was restocking my last booth there, just before our McDonald's stop. Not a good feeling. I just couldn't imagine that I would've not noticed it lying on the floor there. Again, I checked every pocket on me to see if I perhaps slipped it into another pocket for some reason, but it just wasn't there. Nothing. I paused for a moment, took a deep breath, trying not to panic.

I know what, I thought. *When Malinda comes back out, I'll use her phone and dial my phone. Surely, whoever might have found it will answer it and I could ask them to return it.*

Seemed like ages for Malinda to come out of McDonald's. I could hardly wait for her phone.

Oh no. I just thought of something. The ringer on my phone doesn't work anymore. Only my vibrator was working at the moment. Working in this steel fabricating shop, small fine steel dust had collected in the little magnets in my phone speakers and disabled my ringer.

Oh, this is just pitiful.

While waiting there, I searched all around me again to see if the phone was lying anywhere on the floor of the van or somewhere beside me on my seat, but it just wasn't anywhere to be found.

Then a thought just came to my mind. I had not prayed yet. I was trying to find this phone on my own, and this should work, right? If it was lying anywhere close by, I should be able to find it pretty easily. Most likely, this thing got lost while I was at the flea market and someone found it and could make all kinds of long-distance calls and run up my phone bill, I thought.

Wouldn't hurt to pray. There was one thing for sure, I know, and that was wherever this phone was, God knows every thought I have. He even knows I'm all nerved up because I lost my cell phone. Whether he wants me to find it or not, that I don't know, but I can at least pray and ask.

Seek and ye shall find, right?

So I prayed just a short little prayer, acknowledging to God that I know He knows exactly where my cell phone was. In my prayer I said, "I know You could help me locate it if you wanted to, and I ask that You would do that, in Jesus's name." My prayer was just short but to the point. I've had enough small prayers answered that I knew the Lord loves when we ask for His help.

Lo and behold, the *very* next place I reached to check, I reached back around my backside, by my back and the van seat, and there, right there, I felt the phone. My coat was curled up on the inside, making a gutter along the backside, and that phone was lying in that gutter of my coat. So what was happening earlier on, I figured, was whenever I moved around in the van while searching, the phone moved right around with me also.

But I mean to say within seconds of praying, I had found it. In fact, I think it was the very first place my hands reached to after having prayed. I was just about in disbelief. Just absolutely blows my mind, yet I know God can do anything. I experienced this over and over.

This was another affirmation for me that God is real, and He does care about even the little things in our life. It really helps me to stay in tune with the Lord.

It would be very easy for me to think, *Yeah, right, I would've found it anyway without praying.* That's what Satan would like for us to think. But I choose to believe our Lord wants us to ask in His name all the time.

Chapter 21

Final Thoughts

As I think of sharing my life story with the world, I look back and I think of it this way. It was fun and scary all at the same time to write my story. If that makes any sense. Not sure I know how to put it in better words, because every one of us has a story to tell. We all do. My story was not pretty. My past was not pretty. But I rejoice that I no longer have to live in my past. I live for the future. And my hope is that you, too, along with me, can rejoice with me or anyone else who returns to the Lord from their former ways of living, rather than further bringing hurts and pain to their life, you will rejoice with us. And this is why I wanted to share my story with you. If you are someone who can identify with my story and you feel like your life was so horrible that God could never forgive you, remember, it's not God who has you believe this lie. That is a lie straight from the devil himself. He wants you to believe you can never be good enough for God to love you ever again. That you can never be forgiven. Just remember this, Jesus is there with his hands reaching out for you. All you have to do is take his hand in yours.

For me, I did not have the strength to do it on my own. Maybe you can't either. Maybe you need someone to walk beside you for a while. That's where I was. That place for me was Fresh Start. I have learned to trust the staff there, and they helped me pray through some hard things. Things I had done in my life that I wanted to lay to rest so that I could find freedom and peace in my heart and know that Jesus forgave me for my past sins. I did not know how to come to that place on my own. Maybe you do. If you do, praise the Lord. God is faithful to forgive us of our sins, if we are sincere about repenting of those dark areas in our lives.

As I have explained earlier on in my story here, it was hard for me to accept the fact that I needed to go to a place like Fresh Start, but today, I'm not ashamed to admit it, for me, it was where I received a lot of help, and for that, I will forever be grateful. We all need friends like this, willing to walk along our side, to hear us out, and to give good advice. Not to tear us down, but to lift each other up. Too often, we would rather tear the other person down. To make them feel the pain. To make them pay for their wrongs they'd done. This type of attitude will get you nowhere, and later on, it's God who will have to deal with you also. Let us build each other up for the better, in love and respect that we all long for.

Going through Fresh Start was very good for me, and I hope I came through that way in my story. I did not sugarcoat my experience going through the program nor just tell the bad parts of it. So in my story here, when it felt to you like I was pretty hard on my counselor at times, I want you to know I also had good days with him. I will admit, for a lack of better words, I did not always feel loved by him, but that's okay. Today, we are still good friends. I appreciate Jesse's friendship and would wash his feet as Jesus taught us to do. I simply wrote my story as best as I could, and I would never discourage anyone from going through the program at Fresh Start. In fact, it would be quite the opposite. I would encourage you to go. When God calls you there, go. If I could get help there, let me assure you, you can too, I promise. But your heart has to be in it, lean on God, not your counselor. Can you pass the test that God put in front of you?

Today, we, as a family, love to spend time together as much as time allows, and one of those favorite family times is in Sarasota, Florida, over Christmastimes. We've made it our family tradition to have our Christmas in Florida for the past eight or nine years now. Lots of memories made there.

Our prayers are that we can remain faithful to our Lord and Savior Jesus Christ. If you feel encouraged to write me a letter, I would love that. Here is my mailing address:

Nealie Miller

PO Box 6
Montgomery, IN 47558

Or simply write me on my email address, which is Nealiemiller@yahoo.com.

If you enjoyed my story, please tell your friends, maybe they, too, will buy my book. If you didn't enjoy it, keep your mouth shut and tell nobody.😊

*****

I would like to introduce the other book I wrote, *Mike and Ike: The Runaway Boys.* I started writing this book back when we were first married, but it took me many years to get it finished. I got it professionally printed, but I did it the self-publish way. I think you will enjoy this book very much as well. For the most part, my life growing up at home, I believe my dad and I got along pretty good. But of course, we had our arguments also. I got many spankings from my dad, and I'm not going to say I didn't deserve a lot of them, I probably did, but it often felt like Dad did it out of anger at times. And there was this one time that we had this heated disagreement, and I threatened to run away back in the woods and live like the Indians did. I even had a longing to do that. Dreamed about it even. When I made that comment to my dad, he simply told me that I can go, but not to come back looking for food if I got hungry. That scared me, because what if? Well, I never ran away from home. But I wrote the story *Mike and Ike* which bounced off my desires to leave and run away. Mike and Ike ran away from home in their teenage years when they got themselves in a heap of trouble. They ran away, thinking life would be all hunky-dory back in the mountains, but what they didn't realize was, trouble followed them all the way back in the deep forest. They lived peacefully back there for around three years when suddenly, disaster struck them and life would never be the same for Mike and Ike ever again. One morning, Ike was not in his bed. Ike was nowhere to be found. Would Mike ever see Ike ever again? How in the world did he just disappear during the night? A year later, Mike was so lonesome back there alone that he ventured off to look for Ike and to go back home to repent to his parents. One of the hardest things he was facing in life, except he would never make it home. At least not yet. When he finally came upon this real old house at the edge of the woods, still far back in the mountains, the porch roof sagging, the front porch floor caved in. Mike was tired and decided to go see if he could rest in this house. Just before he turned the doorknob, Mike decided maybe he should first knock, just in case. Certainly didn't appear like anyone lived here for years already. Mike had barely knocked when the doorknob turned and the door opened. Life would never be the same for Mike ever again. Follow the wild adventure of Mike and Ike in this story. You'll love it.

Order your copy of Mike and Ike for $12.95 per book plus $3.50 for postage. A 286-page softcover book. Or my 60-page hand-drawn picture coloring book that I put together, for $2.50 plus $3.00 for postage.

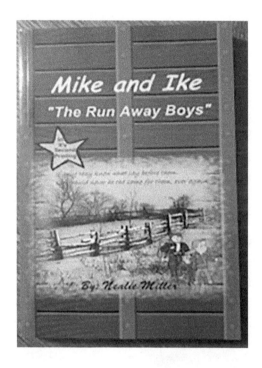

About the Author

Nealie lives in Montgomery, Indiana, with his beautiful wife, Malinda, and still has two children living at home. They have seven healthy children altogether. Their youngest is already seventeen years old, so they can pretty much take care of themselves while Malinda and Nealie travel a lot with the buses nowadays. They get to see a lot of country, a lot of stuff they would never get to see if it wasn't for their travels. They enjoy what they do, but they also enjoy their days at home very much. Nealie loves gardening, but because of all their travels, he doesn't have time for that, but he also enjoys landscaping around home, and he gets to do some of that. Flowers—the more, the merrier.

When he's not on the road, he's often home cleaning or working on his buses. Evenings at home, he's often found reading someone else's book and life story, or he's on his computer, writing. He enjoys writing. If you liked this story, make sure you get a hold of his other book, *Mike and Ike: The Runaway Boys*. You'll enjoy it as well.

His hobby is being in his little woodworking shop refurbishing old furniture and making it look new or antique-like, for resale.

He will likely be writing a follow-up book about himself, but hopefully in a much better light than this one. It may be his story of traveling across the United States in their three-wheeled motorcycle that they don't even have yet, but have dreams of. Most of all, he wants his story to be an inspiration to you and give you hope like he found hope. God bless each one of you.

Printed in the USA
CPSIA information can be obtained
at www.ICGtesting.com
LVHW041942300124
770045LV00001B/70